Understanding Hallyu

This book sheds light on aspects of the Korean Wave and Korean media products that are less discussed—Korean literature, webtoon, and mukbang. It explores the making of these Korean popular cultural products and how they work and engage media recipients regardless of their different national, cultural, and geographical backgrounds.

Drawing on narrative theory and cultural studies, the book makes a compelling argument about how to analyze the production and consumption of Korean media within and beyond its national boundary with critical eyes. The author shows how transmedial narrative studies (narrative studies across media) offers analytical and theoretical lenses through which one can interpret new and emerging media forms and contents. Furthermore, she explores how these forms and contents can be better understood when they are contextualized within specific time and place using the cultural, social, and political concepts and precepts of the region.

The volume will be of great interest to scholars and researchers of Asian Studies, popular culture, contemporary cyberculture, media and culture studies, and literary theory.

Hyesu Park received her PhD in English from Ohio State University in 2014 and is currently an associate professor of English at Bellevue College, Bellevue, WA. In 2015 and 2016, she was a visiting professor at FLAME University, Pune, India. Her research interests include American and Asian-American literatures, narrative theory, media studies, and South Korean literature and popular culture. Her articles have appeared in *Image and Narrative*, *Studies in Twentieth and Twenty-First Century Literature*, and *American Book Review*. Most recently, she edited *Media Culture in Transnational Asia: Convergences and Divergences*. Currently, she is working on a monograph, *Narrating Other Minds: Alterity and Empathy in Post-1945 Asian American Literature* (forthcoming).

"Hyesu Park presents innovative and distinctive approaches in understanding less-privileged areas in the transnationality of the Korean Wave. By uniquely positioning herself as literary scholar, she aptly analyzes three different forms of popular culture, literature, webtoon, and mukbang within the genealogy of Korean literature. Her unique and rich research provides new insights on the convergence of narrative, media, and Korea, which is rare, but makes the book valuable and enjoyable."

— Dal Yong Jin, *Distinguished SFU Professor at Simon Fraser University, Canada*

"The export of Korean culture around the world is one of the most salient transmedial influences in the 21st century. In this path-breaking work, Dr. Park examines digital and cultural forces that have shaped and filtered the rise of the Korean Wave. Through a novel application of narrative theory, she examines webtoons, graphic narratives, fiction and mukbang videos to display how global audiences have come to feel, imagine, think and identify with Korean popular culture. By using semiotic and technical approaches, Dr. Park demonstrates how the digital circulation and remix culture of Korean media has produced inclusive storyworlds for a global audience. *Understanding Hallyu: The Korean Wave Through Literature, Webtoon, and Mukbang* provides a perceptive account of the network effect of a dramatic new addition to Asian cultural studies."

— Maya Dodd, *Assistant Dean of Teaching, Learning, and Engagement at FLAME University, India*

Understanding Hallyu
The Korean Wave Through
Literature, Webtoon, and Mukbang

Hyesu Park

LONDON AND NEW YORK

First published 2021
by Routledge
2 Park Square, Milton Park, Abingdon, Oxon OX14 4RN

and by Routledge
52 Vanderbilt Avenue, New York, NY 10017

Routledge is an imprint of the Taylor & Francis Group, an informa business

© 2021 Hyesu Park

The right of Hyesu Park to be identified as author of this work has been asserted by her in accordance with sections 77 and 78 of the Copyright, Designs and Patents Act 1988.

All rights reserved. No part of this book may be reprinted or reproduced or utilised in any form or by any electronic, mechanical, or other means, now known or hereafter invented, including photocopying and recording, or in any information storage or retrieval system, without permission in writing from the publishers.

Trademark notice: Product or corporate names may be trademarks or registered trademarks, and are used only for identification and explanation without intent to infringe.

British Library Cataloguing-in-Publication Data
A catalogue record for this book is available from the British Library

Library of Congress Cataloging-in-Publication Data
A catalog record has been requested for this book

ISBN: 978-0-367-14358-9 (hbk)
ISBN: 978-1-003-14011-5 (ebk)

Typeset in Times New Roman
by Newgen Publishing UK

Contents

Acknowledgments vi

Introduction 1

1 Korean literature wave: transcultural and transnational reading of *The Vegetarian* and *Bad Friend* 25

2 Korean webtoon wave: narratological, technological, and medial innovations of Korean digital comics 53

3 Korean mukbang wave: making sense of eating and broadcasting and its techno-mediated narrative environment 81

Index 99

Acknowledgments

As a student, teacher, and scholar of literature and narrative theory, I am first and foremost indebted to my professors and mentors, Dr. David Herman, Dr. James Phelan, and Dr. Frederick Aldama, for their teaching and guidance. My training in narrative studies has given me exciting analytical tools and theoretical frames to study Korean media and popular culture.

I would like to thank my home institution, Bellevue College, for the sabbatical leave. The leave allowed me to work on this book with the comfort of time. I also thank my editor Aakash Chakrabarty and his team at Routledge India. Aakash and his team made the process of working on this book smooth, enjoyable, and rewarding. I thank deeply, too, Dr. Dal Yong Jin and Dr. Maya Dodd for their generous endorsements for the book.

I would also like to acknowledge that I was motivated to work on this book after completing an anthology, *Media Culture in Transnational Asia: Convergences and Divergences* (Rutgers University Press, 2020) (for which I was an editor). Some of the researches I referred to in that book are mentioned in the introduction of this book.

Lastly but perhaps most importantly, I am grateful to my mom and dad in Korea for their unconditional love, trust, and support. I dedicate this book to them.

Introduction

The spread of South Korean (hereafter Korean/Korea) popular culture across borders, that is, the Korean Wave or *hallyu*,[1] whose origin dates back to the late 1990s, is no longer a new phenomenon to media users and scholars of media, communications, cultural, and narrative studies alike. Nevertheless, while much attention has been paid to the cross-border dissemination, appropriation, and consumption of Korean television dramas and popular music, much less ink has been spilled on what I am interested in discussing in this book—Korean literature in translation, webtoon (Korean term for digital comics), and *mukbang* (eating and broadcasting), as well as their production and consumption within and beyond the national boundary of Korea. In cases where these media/cultural products are discussed and studied, the focus is often on highlighting the larger cultural, social, and technological background of modern Korean society and its impact on these products in the context of globalization, digitalization, and media convergence and remediation.[2]

My approach to Korean literature, webtoon, and mukbang in this book is based on an a posteriori rather than an a priori method. Instead of declaring broadly what they do and how they do it, I seek to understand the variety of things they do and the variety of ways they do it—analyzing the specific ways in which these media are semiotically, technically, and culturally constituted and mediated, and how their respective media environments influence media recipients within and across borders cognitively, emotionally, psychologically, and ethically. My aim in the book is to shed light on aspects of the Korean Wave and Korean media products that are less discussed and to help familiarize readers with the specific making of them—and to ultimately make clear why and how they work and engage media recipients regardless of their different national, cultural, and geographical backgrounds. Readers who are already somewhat familiar with Korean popular culture will get to know about Korean media and culture that have been relatively less exposed. For those readers who are new to Korean popular culture, this book will function as a useful introductory guide to Korea and its media culture and industry. Before I delve into the selective examples of Korean literature, webtoon, and mukbang, I offer in this introduction some general information about the Korean Wave and justification for my narratologically[3] oriented approach to Korean media and their spread.

Korean media and the Korean Wave: how and why has Korean popular culture reached the globe?

Media can be generally thought of as the means of mass communication as well as the material or form used by artist, composer, writer, or anyone who wishes to communicate, express, or entertain. The focus on the material and form in the conceptualization of media invites considerations for semiotic (image, language, sound) and technology (media-defining features), as they contribute to shaping and filtering media contents and the ways in which media recipients consume, disseminate, and appropriate them. Indeed, a widespread trend in media studies, especially in the English-speaking North, consists of "associating media with specific technologies of communication, such as writing, film, photography, TV, radio, the telephone, and all the uses of digital technology known as 'new media.'"[4] What is left behind in this technologically oriented approach to media, however, are the culturally relevant narrative forms and the understanding of media as regional and cultural practices informed by and informing behaviors, thoughts, and feelings of the people producing and consuming them in specific times and places. This culturally informed and sensitive approach to media is inevitable now given the development and spread of digital and networked media, of which Asia has a significant part.[5]

According to the 2019 statistics from the Internet World Stats, 50.1 percent of the world's Internet population, which amounts to 2.2 billion users in total, is concentrated in Asia.[6] It is thus not surprising that "Chinese, Japanese, Arabic, and Korean are among the top ten most used languages on the web," while Chinese speakers alone "form almost a quarter (23.2%) of the world's Internet population."[7] In the meantime, South Korea is leading the world in the semiconductors industry that is essential to the production of microelectronics.[8] India, on the other hand, is the world's largest exporter of information technology. The digital revolution in Asia is empowered by the rapid economic growth of the region, proactive and decisive government policies,[9] and relatively younger and more technophilic consumers—and these factors are causing fundamental shifts in the existing cultural, economic, and political systems of the region. The results, as Sun Sun Lim and Cheryll Ruth R. Soriano point out, are a "boost in domestic innovation in information technology (IT), considerable growth in the quantity and quality of the region's IT clusters, and a thriving start-up ecosystem," which together generate "trend-setting innovations in social media, online games, mobile commerce, and mobile health" among other things.[10] Undoubtedly, Asia as a whole is instigating new ways of life and spreading innovations across and beyond the region.

Korea, with the world's second-fastest average mobile Internet speeds[11] and the highest rate of smartphone ownership,[12] is one of the leading nations in Asia bringing about these very "trend-setting innovations" in a wide range of media and technology, produced and consumed inside and outside the country. This is in spite of the fact that just 65 years ago Korea was a war-devastated country that depended upon relief supplies from more developed nations of the world. South Korea's per capita gross domestic product (GDP), for instance, was $156 in 1960 but rose to $36,776 in 2018.[13] This explosive economic growth was largely facilitated by "compressed modernity," a form and condition for modernization where cultural, social, political, and economic changes take place in an extremely compressed manner in terms of both space and time, leading to "the construction and reconstruction of a highly complex and fluid social system."[14] Indeed, South Korea achieved significant economic and social changes and development over the course of just half a century after the end of Japanese colonization (1910–1945) and civil war (1950–1953) and during military rule and the authoritarian regimes (1961–1993). Of course, these rapid and authoritatively administered economic, industrial, and social changes brought the nation ambiguities, imbalances, and inequalities, leaving many domains of society "unattended, underdeveloped, protracted, or distorted."[15] Nevertheless, the compressed process of modernization of Korea required the nation to be flexible, innovative, efficient, and fluid. The rapid development of the country and society has also made Koreans proud, confident, and diligent, motivating them to devote themselves to national and individual advancement. For instance, the 2019 enrollment rate of eligible students at South Korean universities was 67.8 percent[16] while, according to 2016 data compiled by the Organization for Economic Co-operation and Development (OECD), South Korea has "longer working hours than any other developed country: an average 2,069 hours per year, per worker."[17] All these social, cultural, and national elements and characteristics of Korea have provided the foundation for the nation to establish itself as a leader in the global media and technological landscape.

Korea started exporting its own media products to Asia (mostly China and Japan) in the late 1990s. The term Korean Wave was also coined during this time. Although the initial stage of the Korean Wave focused primarily on exporting television dramas to neighboring nations, it now includes a wider range of Korean media and cultural products—popular music (K-pop), films, online games, sports (sports players), cosmetics (lifestyle more broadly), food, and even language—and has reached many other nations further away from Korea—the United States, Europe, and the Middle East to name but a few. Most notably, K-pop has garnered enthusiastic responses from many fans across the globe thanks to its catchy melodies, musical themes that are easy to sing and hum along to, elaborate dance routines, and music videos with artistic and bold visuals. Music video for "Gangnam Style," released in 2012 by Korean rapper and singer Psy, for instance, hit 3 billion views on YouTube in 2019, while the boy band BTS, launched in 2012, became the first K-pop band to top the US album charts and has more than 12 million subscribers on YouTube (as of 2019).[18] When seen within this global context, the Korean Wave phenomenon can be thought of as a creation of "regional 'Asian' cultural manifestation against the erstwhile domination of Western culture"[19] and a way to "counter the threat and insensibility of the Western-dominated media market within the context of global inequalities and uneven power structures."[20] Indeed, the Korean Wave offers a platform for what Kuan Hsing Chen calls "Asia as method" in which "using Asia as an imaginary anchoring point can allow societies in Asia to become one another's reference points so that the understanding of the self can be transformed and subjectivity rebuilt."[21] The rise of the Korean Wave across the globe allows Korea to become the very reference and anchoring point for not only the nations within Asia but also those outside Asia. Through the understanding of the Korean Wave, Korea's own subjectivity can be rebuilt (from the Morning Calm to the global cultural and techno hub), the pan-Asian identity can be restructured through the lens of "pop Asianism,"[22] and understanding of the West and globalization as a Western cultural force can be de-Westernized and de-parochialized.[23]

A few factors have contributed to the rise of the Korean Wave. As Youna Kim in her introduction to *The Korean Wave: Korean Media Go Global* notes, Korea's export of popular media culture was initiated by the government at the time of the 1997 Asian financial crisis as "a new economic initiative, one of the major sources of foreign revenue vital for the country's economic survival and advancement."[24] The strategic governmental effort did not disappoint, as Korean cultural content exports increased from $500 million in 2000–2002 to $800 million in 2004. Since then, exports rose exponentially, reaching $4.42 billion in 2010.[25] According to the 2018 report by Hyundai Research Institute (HRI), the boy band BTS alone generated "4 trillion won ($3.54 billion) as economic value to the country per year and 1.42 trillion won ($1.26 billion) as added value per year."[26] In the same 2018 report, HRI also estimated that "BTS's ten-year economic impact will reach 56.2 trillion won ($49.8 billion)."[27] The popularity of Korean pop music, drama, and film naturally leads to the increasing popularity of individual artists and performers, and the Korean Wave consumers' desire to look and dress like them. For instance, as a Korean individual living in the United States, I often face the question, "How do all these Koreans on television look so thin, well-dressed, and pretty?" Such a question, while being anecdotal and overly generalizing, is too significant to ignore. For instance, "lookism," a term used to refer to the attitude of privileging physical attractiveness, is especially widespread and deeply rooted in modern Korean society.[28] According to the 2015 survey by Nielsen Korea, conducted online with 3 million people from 60 different countries, 6 out of 10 Koreans answered that they thought themselves to be overweight, marking higher (60 percent) than the global average of 49 percent. This is striking especially given that Korea has the lowest overweight rate among all OECD (the Organization for Economic Cooperation and Development) nations. It is also notable that one out of two Koreans is regularly on a diet, rigorously controlling his or her daily food consumption.[29] The extreme lookism of Korean society leads to many severe problems, such as eating disorders and excessive bodybuilding and exercises, but has also contributed to the global spread of and aspirations for the Korean-lifestyle. The Korean beauty industry, for instance, is among the top 10 around the globe, with an estimated worth of over $13.1 billion in sales in 2018 alone.[30]

Another important factor contributing to the success of the Korean Wave may lie in the emotional relevance and resonance that Korean popular culture seems to evoke in the minds of audiences around the world. Youna Kim, for instance, in speaking of the popular Korean television dramas in particular, calls this emotional experience "A-ha! Emotion," "an emotional resolution and closure in the experience of the relevant and recognizable forms of popular culture."[31] Although the sudden and yet gradual rise of the Korean Wave has left many observers in a state of surprise and bewilderment, Kim notes that the most common response from fans of Korean dramas is that they are "emotionally powerful." Interviews with experts and overseas fans of these dramas clearly show how emotion plays a significant role in various transnational locations: "The unique intensity of Korean emotion plays well to the more restrained cultures around the region"; "[Chinese audiences particularly enjoy Korean dramas because of the ways in which Koreans in these dramas] express their emotions freely, that it is a democracy"; "If there was ever such a man [male protagonists in Korean dramas who are sensitive and caring towards women] in Japan, I wouldn't be suffering like this."[32] Although the exact nature of and reasons for these responses differ, the fact that these media users are emotionally aroused regardless of their region and culture indicates strongly that "[t]here is no such thing as human culture or human cultural difference without human universality."[33] Indeed, Patrick Hogan posits that verbal art (and to some extent, any form of art) of any region and culture involves "all varieties of emotions"[34] that are not necessarily narrowly egocentric but empathetic. What is important to note here is that empathetic emotion, which, according to Hogan, verbal art universally aims to evoke in the minds of the audiences, can be triggered either by the situational particularity or group identity. That is, we share someone else's emotion "in so far as we have been in a parallel situation" or because "we tacitly understand him or her as sharing our identity."[35] Hogan concludes that, although specifics of emotional situations and group identities vary from culture to culture, "the general principles governing empathetic emotion ... are cross-culturally constant."[36]

The universal human capacity to feel empathetic emotions for others (including for fictional characters) allows the overseas audiences of Korean popular cultural products to feel for and relate to what they read, watch, or listen to regardless of their own widely different cultural, regional, ethnic, and linguistic backgrounds. In fact, linguistic commonality seems to be the least important factor when it comes to the popularity of the Korean Wave. After all, thousands of people at concerts by Korean boy or girl bands screaming their hearts out in a language that they have no idea about is no longer an unusual scene. Experts and fans of K-pop attribute its success to its non-linguistic aspects, such as music videos, elaborate choreography, attractive appearance of the artists, catchy melodies and rhythms as well as the overall message of the songs (rather than the specific lyrics), and so forth. Whether the audience fully understands the meaning of the songs or not, these songs leave upbeat and positive feelings in people's minds and create an overall "sensory experience"[37] that people, regardless of their cultural or linguistic backgrounds, come to feel, share, and therefore understand. This emotion-universal approach alone, of course, cannot fully explain the why and how of the Korean Wave. Rather, it shows that the intended audience for certain media and cultural products is far exceeded. While dissemination is unpredictable, it is only natural when media and cultural products of a particular nation are adapted elsewhere in new contexts and forms. What catches the fancy of which national mood is anyone's guess. Such global practices of transgression and adaptation of media and culture are reconstituting the boundedness of regions and question the very stability of categories of identity. What is important to note, then, is that the success of the Korean Wave meaningfully reflects that culture and cultural identity that inform and are informed by media are no longer restricted by geographical and national boundaries. More importantly, perhaps, it speaks to the much-needed urge to challenge the one-way cultural flow from the West to the rest. The Korean Wave successfully participates in the effort to decentralize the Western-centric cultural force and flow.

Lastly, the development of the Internet and digital technology in general has significantly empowered the dissemination of popular cultural and media products of Korea. The technologies of the Internet and mobile communication interlink people across geographic borders. The outcome, as Eugenia Siapera points out, is the diminished relevance of the nation-state, as people are able to be "connected and brought together in a space outside their real or imaginary homeland."[38] Manuel Castells further conceptualizes this space "outside their real or imaginary homeland" as "network society." According to Castells, the rise of the network in new technologically advanced societies has given birth to a new notion of space based "not on physical proximity but on the exchange of flows."[39] The network society free from any physical proximity mobilizes and reorganizes its actors and their activities in strikingly new ways and in a space not of places but of flows.[40] Moreover, within this space of flows and exchanges, ethnicity or race, while never ceasing to exist, are neither bound to specific territories nor providing "the basis for a common identity." As Castells further elaborates, in network society, "ethnic roots are twisted, divided, reprocessed, mixed, differentially stigmatized, or rewarded, according to a new logic of informationalization and globalization of cultures and economies that makes symbolic composites out of blurred identities. Race matters, but it hardly constructs meaning any longer."[41] The advent of "network society" interlinks distant geographic locations and enables Korean cultural and media products to rapidly cross borders and to be consumed and reappropriated by audiences of widely different ethnic and racial roots.

Korea's own digital industry has undoubtedly fostered the advancement of media culture of Korea and its global spread. Korea's digitalization was initiated by the government in the early 1990s with policies "designed to restructure the national economy" and create a significant shift "from a dependence on manufacturing to an export-oriented, service-based knowledge economy in which creative and cultural industries play a major part."[42] Accordingly, the government set up Korea Information Infrastructure (KII) in March 1995 with a goal of establishing an advanced nationwide information infrastructure "consisting of communications networks, Internet services, application software, computers, and information products and services."[43] The construction of the nation's knowledge-based economy orchestrated by KII can be divided into three phases: the first phase (1996–2000) aiming at laying the foundation; the second phase (2001–2005) focusing on encouraging the use of information networks; and the third and last phase (2006–2010) promoting a higher level of information network use.[44] In 2020, Korea led the global race to deploy 5G, "with 85 of more than 100 cities in the country now connected, [and placing itself] ahead of China, the US and UK, which counted 57, 50, and 31 connected cities, respectively."[45] The introduction of the smartphone, on the other hand, has brought about further changes in the sociocultural and economic environments of Korea. According to Dal Yong Jin, the start of Korea's wireless communications service dates back to 1984. Yet the number of smartphone users spiked significantly in 2015. By the end of August the same year, smartphone subscription rates reached 79.6 percent (out of the 53.2 million mobile subscriptions in total), "up from around 1.6% of total mobile phone users in December 2009."[46] The high smartphone penetration rates of the country have led to the development of other cultural industries, including, for instance, mobile games (Korea's mobile game market was valued at $2.34 billion in 2017[47]) and webtoons (online comics, which I discuss in detail in the second chapter of this book), and intersects with other areas of the society, accelerating in particular political participations of young Koreans.[48]

With the advent and development of the Internet, digitization of the society, and new social media came the evolution of the relationship among media producers/industry stakeholders, artists, and fans. The role that fans take in this new relationship has been quintessential to the global dissemination of the Korean Wave. Web 2.0 platforms, such as YouTube, Facebook, and Twitter, with their synergetic and proliferating nature as well as open-source image-making software, have lowered the barrier for the creation and dissemination of media contents. As these platforms offer an ease of content uploading and sharing, fans are now figured as "prosumers" who invest their affective labor to contribute ideas and improvements to professional media production or to create their own user-generated contents. As Henry Jenkins has said, "fans of all forms of popular culture have not only been consumers, but they are also producers of culture who modify, extend and expand the bounds of pop culture texts and narratives."[49] Such fan participations and activities have, as Dorothy Wai Sim Lau points out, escalated professionalization of the amateur, collapsing "the dividing line between the professional and the amateur" and validating "the trend that popular texts no longer stay in the cultural terrain as [they] used to, but move across diverse media platforms, driven by both the mainstream industrial initiative and the alternative business initiative."[50] These initiatives that mobilize and empower fans are evident on, for instance, Soompi, one of the biggest online K-pop communities with around 22 million users (as of 2018). The vast majority of these users are not Koreans, but they voluntarily spend hours translating and analyzing Korean lyrics and sharing their translations with other fans on the community. These fans also search, copy, and appropriate other visual productions (interviews, for instance) sourced from mainstream media and share their own amateur productions of remixes and mashups, actively joining the co-create culture of many amateur-friendly websites.

Among such websites is YouTube, which can be confidently said to be the best friend to the Korean Wave in general and K-pop in particular. YouTube was founded in 2005 and is the dominant platform for online video sharing worldwide today, "having experienced rapid growth in both audience share and in the amount of content uploaded."[51] Although YouTube first started as an open online cultural space for amateur video making and uploading, it has gradually evolved to expedite professionalization and formalization of amateur media production, functioning as a "commercial platform built on both amateur and professional content and supported by advertising," as well as "the new commercial cultural intermediaries that specialize in first marketing and then professionalizing 'amateur' YouTube activity."[52] Notably, YouTube includes K-pop in their music category, which consists of other music genres such as R&B, rap, pop, rock, and so forth. K-pop is "the first genre to be created for a particular country" on YouTube.[53] The YouTube topical page for K-pop,[54] for instance, has 1.51 million subscribers (as of 2020). Major K-pop producers, such as SM Entertainment and YG Entertainment, use this page to advertise their music and encourage audiences to freely download and share their professionally produced media contents. Fans further appropriate these contents into their own amateur remakes. All videos on this page also have comment streams and enable fans to share their feedback and eventually build up virtual communities, which are essential when it comes to the popularity and spread of K-pop. Indeed, the "virality" of K-pop videos on YouTube, commented on and shared actively by and among fans, has played "a crucial marketing, distributional and advertising role in promoting K-pop as a popular entertainment worldwide."[55] Thanks to the growth of content-sharing and video uploading websites such as YouTube and others, as well as the reciprocal relationships between fans and media producers on the one hand and among the individual members of fan networks on the other hand, audiences (domestic and global) of Korean popular culture can easily access a wide range of contents that will further fuel their enthusiasm, curiosity, and creativity for the Korean culture and media.

Narratological approach to Korean literature, webtoon, and mukbang video

There are three key elements that are interrelated and govern the construction of the present book: narrative, media, and Korea. Narrative or narrative text can be broadly understood as "one that brings a world to the mind (setting) and populates it with intelligent agents (characters) … a mental representation of causally connected states and events that captures a segment in the history of a world and of its members."[56] Medium, on the other hand, is a channel or a material means of expression, communication, and entertainment. Putting narrative and media together in the context of Korea, then, this book is about the ways in which Korean media products structure narrative and the processes of its production, consumption, and dissemination within and beyond the national boundary of Korea. The book's emphasis on media's narrative potential means that I pay close attention not only to what messages the three distinct types of Korean media under discussion convey but, more importantly, how their different configurations shape and filter what is communicated to media recipients (and how it is communicated) in specific time and place (Korea or elsewhere) and inform their cognitive, affective, and ethical activities and responses. The narratological approach to media in this book can be best captured by what Marie-Laure Ryan says about the choice of medium and its impact on narrative: "The choice of medium makes a difference as to what stories can be told, how they are told, and why they are told. By shaping narrative, media shape nothing less than human experience."[57] Even more simply put, as Marshall McLuhan has famously announced, "the medium is the message," for "the medium determines the modes of perception and the matrix of assumptions within which objectives are set."[58] The intricate relationship between narrative and medium and how Korea as the cultural and social context intersects with this relationship guide my

Introduction   11

discussion in each chapter as I study multiple facets of Korean media semiotically (language, image, sound, and movement), technically (media-defining technologies as well as any kind of mode of production and material support), and culturally (media and narrative as situated practices, informing and being informed by the behaviors and psychology of users, producers, and institutions).[59]

Narratology generally refers to the study of narrative and narrative structure and the ways that they affect human perception. How literary scholars apply narratology to their investigations of narrative texts differs in various ways and with varying emphases. Rhetorical theorists, for instance, conceptualize narrative as "somebody telling somebody else that something happened" and focus on "the multilayered communications that authors of narrative offer their audiences, communications that invite or even require their audiences to engage with them cognitively, psychically, emotionally, and ethically."[60] Cognitive theorists, on the other hand, offer yet another approach to the study of narrative with a process of the audience's mental simulations in mind. For them, narratives represent "worlds that are populated with characters and situated in space and time."[61] These scholars are particularly concerned with the "worlds" evoked by narratives and understand that narrative and narrative comprehension invite narrative recipients to simulate in their minds "mental models of who did what to and with whom, when, where, why, and in what fashion in the world to which recipients relocate."[62] While the conceptualizations of narrative and narratological approach diverge from theorist to theorist, what is common among these varying views is that they are equally concerned with the dynamics between the producer and consumer of narrative, whether the focus is placed on the communicative acts between them or the processes of mental simulations. My use of narrative theory in the study of Korean media, then, is to draw more careful attention to those individuals who mobilize and facilitate media and their narrative potentials. It is also to understand better how the ways in which these individuals behave, think, feel, and evaluate shape the production, consumption, and dissemination of media (and their various consequences and implications) within and beyond the national borders of Korea.

A narratological approach to Korean media with an emphasis on human interaction is especially timely and relevant in the era of the Internet that has generated intrinsically global audiences and where the cross-cultural/border exchanges are more than common. What are the psychological, cognitive, and emotional mechanisms and conditions that make possible cross-cultural acceptance? How do these mechanisms and conditions explain the ways in which multilayered communications and cognitive simulations occur between the foreign entertainment/producer and the audience? How do these communications and simulations override cultural distance and dissonance, leading to aesthetic pleasure commonly enjoyed and celebrated by audiences across the globe? As Young Min Baek in his study of cross-cultural music video consumption on YouTube points out, culturally incongruent objects can cause psychological rewards and aesthetic pleasure in people if "a person perceives such unfamiliarity as cognitively challenging but has sufficient cognitive resources to process the novelty."[63] This conclusion leads to two important areas of inquiry in the study of Korean media: (1) What are the semiotic, cultural, and technical affordances of Korean media products that help activate a person's "cognitive resources," leading to cognitive resonance rather than dissonance in a person? (2) How do the tools of narratology (rhetorical and cognitive, for instance) help make sense of and interpret the nuanced ways in which the cultural or aesthetic incongruency of Korean media products is rendered congruent for the cognitive and affective pleasures of global and domestic audiences?

Researchers of cross-cultural and media studies have been questioning why and how global audiences incorporate cross-border media into their own cultural context and make sense of and attribute their own meaning to them.[64] As one of the key assumptions in cross-cultural studies is that "cultures ... emerge through the processes by which humans interact with and seize meanings and resources from their cultures,"[65] these scholars are often attuned to the ways in which national culture and identity as well as the general socio-historical and political economic backdrop inform fannish pursuits within and beyond borders. This socio-historical and political approach, however, is somewhat outdated when it comes to the new media and their circulation, which have led to the birth of "network society,"[66] and given the new dynamics between media producer and consumer where the audience takes a greater role actively seeking new entertainment in order to disseminate, remix, and ultimately remake it. The audience, in other words, has become the all-powerful agent in the era of the Internet and new digital media. In this regard, shifting the attention from the context to the individuals, who are actively involved in the media/culture production and consumption, is timely and urgent, even while these individuals' minds and bodies are still in part informed by the location where they are physically situated. I hence echo Bertha Chin and Lori Hitchcock Morimoto when they argue in their study of transcultural fandom that any consideration of the ways in which the contradictory, chaotic forces of globalization play out in fandom should proceed not only from [socio-historical and political economic] contexts, but equally from our informed understanding of fan behaviors, motivations, and processes of meaning-making as driven by affective pleasures and investments.[67]

This undeniably applies to the studies of Korean media more broadly, and as I contend in this book, narrative theory can help uncover these very processes of individual media producers' and consumers' meaning-making as well as the cognitive and affective exchanges between them that drive and structure today's media landscape.

My analysis of Korean literature, webtoon, and YouTube mukbang channel in this book is hence informed by the various tools of narratology that aim to explain more precisely the specific and yet nuanced ways in which media are constructed and engage users cognitively, affectively, psychically, and ethically. These tools and concepts will also illuminate how media users make sense of and attribute meaning to what they read, view, and hear, and how the semiotics, technology, and culture that constitute media influence these sense-making processes for media users. While I provide detailed definitions and explanations for all narratological terms and concepts whenever I use them, it is worthwhile to briefly re-emphasize two branches of narrative theory—rhetorical and cognitive—and how they relate to my study of Korean media in this book. The rhetorical theory of narrative, especially that of James Phelan, assumes narrative as an event, "a multidimensional purposive communication from a teller to an audience."[68] Rhetorical theorists are therefore interested in uncovering how the teller shapes narrative as a structured sign system in the service of his/her larger ends and investigate narrative's "affective, ethical, and aesthetic effects—and in their intersections—as it is in that narrative's thematic meanings."[69] Media, when considered as contents/narratives configured in various forms with a wide range of semiotic, technical, and cultural components, can also be understood as purposive communications from the author to the audience with specific effects on the audience's cognitive, affective, and ethical responses and activities. Equally relevant is the notion of the authorial audience in the rhetorical model. The rhetorical approach theorizes the authorial audience as "the hypothetical group for whom the author writes—the group that shares the knowledge, values, prejudices, fears, and experiences that the author expected in his or her readers, and that ground his or her rhetorical choices."[70] While different audiences interpret and experience narrative differently, the authorial audience and its interpretation are what rhetorical theorists and I are interested in. The rhetorical theory of narrative and its communicative model, with the authorial audience's interpretation and experience at the center, guide my analysis in this book as I investigate and question: (1) How does the specific construction of a certain media product reflect the purpose and intention of the author/producer/entertainer? (2) What and how do the semiotic, technical, and cultural components of the media product help the author to invite his/her audience to take the position of his/her authorial audience? (3) How, especially in the case of new digital media, do the audience's cognitive, affective, and ethical responses reshape the communicative dynamics between the author and the audience? After all, as Toby Miller and Marwan Kraidy assert, "everyone is creative and no one is a spectator. ... [E]ach people is a consumer on the one hand, but also a producer."[71]

In addition to the rhetorical approach to narrative, I take seriously, too, the cognitive approach to narrative. Cognitive narrative theorists, as mentioned earlier, consider narratives as representations of worlds populated with characters and situated in time and place. While these theorists are interested in understanding how narratives facilitate and help readers simulate these worlds in their minds, David Herman calls these worlds "storyworlds" and defines them as global mental representations evoked "implicitly as well as explicitly by a narrative, whether that narrative takes the form of a printed text, film, graphic novel, sign language, everyday conversation, or even a tale that is projected but never actualized as a concrete artifact."[72] The concept of storyworld is, in other words, transmedial, although it and the processes of its simulation take widely different forms depending on the specific mediality of a distinct medium. Following are relevant questions to consider in the context of media studies: (1) How is the mental construction of storyworld, that is, "the act of imagination required of the reader, spectator, or player," affected by the type of signs that a medium uses?[73] (2) What are the elements of media and their narratives, intradiegetic (semiotics and technology, for instance) as well as extradiegetic (culture and society), that help evoke storyworlds in the minds of media/narrative recipients? In the rest of the book, I will try to answer these and other questions by studying carefully the various ways in which Korean literature, webtoon, and mukbang video engage readers/viewers within and outside the national border and invite them to think, feel, and imagine in specifically guided ways in order to ultimately encourage them to relocate to the worlds evoked implicitly or explicitly by media for various cognitive, affective, ethical, psychical, and political purposes.

Chapter summary

Chapter 1 examines contemporary Korean literature in English translation, using Han Kang's novel *The Vegetarian*[74] and Ancco's graphic memoir *Bad Friend*[75] as case studies. Through close reading of the two literary texts in English translation, I aim to show elements of their narratives that may have contributed to their popular receptions globally. *The Vegetarian*, for instance, is aesthetically (aesthetic uncanny and striking visual elements), formally (three-part construction with diverse perspectives), and narratologically (use of unnatural narrative and feminist narratology) rich in its construction. Additionally, the novel is thematically timely and universal (ecofeminism, among other things, for instance) while contextually specific simultaneously (set in contemporary South Korea and situated within Korea's patriarchal family dynamics). The consequence is the compelling weaving together of the universal and the particular, which helps to enstrange[76] global readers effectively and renew their perspectives. *Bad Friend*, on the other hand, uses a medium that is relatively freer from the obstacle of translation, that is, graphic narrative, and relies on both the visual and verbal narratives to communicate to readers. *Bad Friend* in particular capitalizes on the graphic medium in order to illustrate what is universally unspeakable, repulsive, and distressing, life of an adolescent growing up with sexual abuse, teen prostitution, violence, and drugs. Whereas "novel reading can be so easily stopped or interrupted by unpleasant emotional reaction to a book,"[77] Ancco's careful visual choices, use of the first-person autobiographical narration and focalization,[78] and the overall lyric quality of the narrative as a dominant mode of progression enhance readers' affective engagement with the narrative and enable them to bear witness to the painful memories illustrated by the author.

Chapter 2 examines webtoon as another significant media and cultural product of South Korea that constitutes the Korean Wave and deserves further analytical and theoretical attention. In my attempt to shed light on the diverse (themes, characters, styles) and innovative (technological, narratological, medium-specific) nature of Korean webtoons, I offer close readings of two individual webtoons, *Dr. P Series* and *Encountered*, and focus on the systematic ways in which these webtoons engage readers and inform their reading experience with their unique technological and narratological properties and medium specificities.

For the *Dr. P Series*, I challenge the popular idea in literary studies that readable fictional minds are crucial to the reading of fiction.[79] I posit that the author of the *Dr. P Series* consciously erases readable minds by making deliberate artistic and narratological choices, and this absence of readable minds is at the center of the new mode of reading that the *Dr. P Series* facilitates through its digital mediality. In my discussion of *Encountered*, on the other hand, I pay greater attention to the techno-mediated narrative environment of the webtoon and its numerous technological innovations. These include, among other things, the use of augmented reality and 360-degree panorama and facial recognition. Ultimately, I show how the webtoon allows readers to step literally into the webtoon's simulated world and makes possible the highly embodied reading experience for readers.

Chapter 3 explores another recent media trend in South Korea, mukbang. Mukbang, meaning in Korean, "eating and broadcasting," is an online audiovisual broadcast in which a host eats food in front of a camera while talking to his/her viewers or remaining silent without any verbal communication. Mukbang was made popular in Korea in the late 2000s by broadcast jockeys (BJs) who started live-streaming their shows wherein they consume large meals by using online live-streaming platforms such as Afreeca TV or YouTube. Some of these shows have an online chat box and allow viewers to directly interact with BJs, making possible real-time communications between the host and viewers. In this chapter, my interest lies specifically in an interactive mukbang show as I consider deeply how the techno-mediated narrative environment of the show informs and even subverts the usual hierarchical dynamics and relationships between narrative/media producer and consumer in such a way that narrative recipients come to take on a more active role, participating in and contributing to the meaning-making process. As in the previous two chapters of the book, I turn to the existing narratological models in order to make sense of the production and consumption of mukbang and how mukbang as a cultural and media product for communication and expression engages viewers. However, the core of current narrative theory is still predominantly concerned with narrative/narrative text wherein verbal structures and content are fixed and deemed unconditional. In using interactive new media situated specifically within a Korean context as a site for narrative investigation, then, my goal is to suggest a move towards media and narrative studies that are culturally informed and fluidly respond to the specificities of time and place, as well as the "textual features of the object of analysis that involve textual conditions"[80] that are simultaneously technical, semiotic, cultural, psychological, and behavioral.

Notes

1. The term *hallyu* was first used in China and can be translated into *the Korean Wave*. It is a collective term that encompasses a wide range of Korean popular culture.
2. See, for instance, *Routledge Handbook of Korean Culture and Society* (New York: Routledge, 2016) and *The Korean Wave: Korean Media Go Global* (New York: Routledge, 2013), both edited by Youna Kim.
3. Narratology, or narrative theory, generally refers to the branch of knowledge or literary criticism that deals with the structure and function of narrative and its themes, conventions, symbols, and effects.
4. Marie Laure-Ryan, "Story/Worlds/Media: Tuning the Instruments of a Media-Conscious Narratology," in *Storyworlds across Media: Towards a Media-Conscious Narratology*, ed. Marie-Laure Ryan and Jan-Noël Thon (Lincoln: University of Nebraska Press, 2014), 27.
5. I discuss in detail the important role that Asia is taking in the development of digital media and industry in the introduction to my recent edited volume, *Media Culture in Transnational Asia: Convergences and Divergences* (New Brunswick: Rutgers University Press, 2020).
6. "Internet Usage Statistics: The Internet Big Picture," *Internet World Stats*, last modified March 31, 2019, www.internetworldstats.com/stats.htm.
7. Sun Sun Lim and Cheryll Ruth R. Soriano, "A (Digital) Giant Awakens—Invigorating Media Studies with Asian Perspectives," in *Asian Perspectives on Digital Culture*, ed. Sun sun Lim and Cheryll Ruth R. Soriano (New York: Routledge, 2016), 3.
8. Samsung Electronics and SK Hynix are the world's largest and third largest suppliers of semiconductors. See "Top-15 Semiconductor Suppliers 2018," *Anysilicon*, August 20, 2018, https://anysilicon.com/top-15-semiconductor-suppliers-2018/.
9. Consider, for instance, Taiwan's technocracy-centered economic planning.
10. Lim and Soriano, "A (Digital) Giant," 4.
11. Jessica Clement, "Countries with the Fastest Average Mobile Internet Speeds as of May 2020," *statista*, June 25, 2020, www.statista.com/statistics/896768/countries-fastest-average-mobile-internet-speeds/.
12. S. O'Dea, "Smartphone Ownership Rate by Country 2018," *statista*, February 27, 2020, www.statista.com/statistics/539395/smartphone-penetration-worldwide-by-country/.
13. "South Korea GDP per capita PPP," *Trading Economics*, last accessed May 5, 2020, https://tradingeconomics.com/south-korea/gdp-per-capita-ppp.
14. Kyung-Sup Chang, "Compressed Modernity in South Korea," in *Routledge Handbook of Korean Culture and Society*, ed. Youna Kim (New York: Routledge, 2016), 33.
15. Ibid., 41.
16. Won So, "Enrollment Rate in University in South Korea from 2009 to 2019," *statista*, June 22, 2020, www.statista.com/statistics/629032/south-korea-university-enrollment-rate/.

18 *Introduction*

17 Fernando Duarte, "Which Country Works the Longest Hours?" *BBC News*, last accessed March 8, 2020, www.bbc.com/worklife/article/20180504-which-country-works-the-longest-hours.
18 Vivek Chaudhary, "Feast from the East—Why Britain is Surfing the Korean Culture Wave," *The Guardian*, April 21, 2019, www.theguardian.com/music/2019/apr/21/feast-from-east-britain-surfing-korean-culture-wave.
19 Jim Dator and Yongseok Seo, "Korea as the Wave of a Future," *Journal of Future Studies* 9 (2004): 33.
20 Youna Kim, "Korean Wave Pop Culture in the Global Internet Age: Why Poplar? Why Now?" in *The Korean Wave: Korean Media Go Global*, ed. Youna Kim (New York: Routledge, 2013), 86.
21 Kuan Hsing Chen, *Asia As Method: Toward Deimperialization* (Durham: Duke University Press, 2010), xv.
22 Kim, "Korean Wave," 80.
23 For more on this approach to de-Westernize, see James Curran and Myung-Jin Park, *De-Westernizing Media Studies* (New York: Routledge, 2000).
24 Youna Kim, "Introduction: Korean Media in a Digital Cosmopolitan World," in *The Korean Wave: Korean Media Go Global*, ed. Youna Kim (New York: Routledge, 2013), 3.
25 Ibid., 5
26 Wandering Shadow, "The 'BTS Effect' on South Korea's Economy, Industry and Culture," *Medium*, May 30, 2019, https://medium.com/@shadow_twts/the-bts-effect-on-south-koreas-economy-industry-and-culture-975e8933da56.
27 Ibid.
28 The term "lookism," referring to a discriminatory treatment toward people considered physically unattractive, was first coined in the 1970s and used in *The Washington Post* magazine in 1978. The word now appears in several major English language dictionaries.
29 "South Korea has the Lowest Overweight among All OECD nations, but!" (my trans.), *Joongang Ilbo* online, last modified January 23, 2015, https://news.joins.com/article/17010069.
30 Marian Liu, "Beyond Beauty: Korean Makeup Provides 'Cosmeceuticals,'" *CNN*, April 11, 2018, www.cnn.com/2018/04/11/health/korean-makeup-beauty-health-benefits/index.html.
31 Kim, "Korean Wave," 76.
32 Ibid., 77. These interviews, sourced from various magazines and articles, appear in Kim's chapter.
33 Patrick Hogan, "Of Literary Universals: Ninety-Five Theses," *Philosophy and Literature* 32, no. 1 (2008): 145.
34 Ibid., 146.
35 Ibid., 146–147.
36 Ibid., 147. For more detailed discussion on the narrative universals and prototypical human emotions, See Patrick Hogan, *The Mind and Its Stories: Narrative Universals and Human Emotions* (Cambridge: Cambridge University Press, 2003).

37 Amy X. Wang, "How K-Pop Conquered the West," *Rolling Stone,* August 21 (2018), www.rollingstone.com/music/music-features/bts-kpop-albums-bands-global-takeover-707139/.
38 Eugenia Siapera, *Cultural Diversity and Global Media* (Oxford: Wiley-Blackwell, 2010), 184.
39 Ibid., 185.
40 Ibid.
41 Manuel Castells, *The Rise of the Network Society* (Oxford: Wiley-Blackwell, 2000), 63.
42 Dal Yong Jin, "How To Understand the Emergence of Digital Korea," in *Routledge Handbook of Korean Culture and Society*, ed. Youna Kim (New York: Routledge, 2016), 183.
43 Ibid.
44 For more detailed explanation, see Sanghoon Lee and Jae-Il Jung, "Telecommunications Markets, Industry, and Infrastructure in Korea," *IEEE Communications Magazine* 36 (11): 59–64.
45 Melanie Mingas, "South Korea Leads 5G deployment," *Capacity*, February 27 (2020), www.capacitymedia.com/articles/3824986/south-korea-leads-5g-deployment.
46 Jin, "How To," 187.
47 Sohn Ji-young, "Korean Market Grows for Online, Mobile Games," *The Korean Herald*, June 20 (2018), www.koreaherald.com/view.php?ud=20180620000648.
48 See Jin for more on this as well as Jiyeon Kang "Coming to Terms with 'Unreasonable' Global Power: The 2002 South Korean Candlelight Vigils," *Communication and Critical/Cultural Studies* 6, no. 2 (2009): 171–192 and Dong-Hoo Lee, "Digital Cameras, Personal Photography and the Reconfiguration of Spatial Experiences," *The Information Society* 26 (2010): 266–275.
49 Matthew Guschwan, "New Media: Online Fandom," *Soccer & Society* 17, no. 3 (2016): 352.
50 Dorothy Wai Sim Lau, "Star Construction in the Era of Media Convergence," in *Media Culture in Transnational Asia: Convergences and Divergences*, ed. Hyesu Park (New Brunswick: Rutgers University Press, 2020), 58.
51 In 2011, the company announced that "the site enjoyed 3 billion views per day and 48 hours of video footage uploaded per minute." For more, see Jean Burgess, "YouTube and the Formalization of Amateur Media," in *Amateur Media: Social, Cultural and Legal Perspectives*, ed. Dan Hunter, Ramon Lobato, Julian Thomas, and Megan Richardson (London: Routledge, 2013): 53.
52 Ibid., 54.
53 Kent A. Ono and Jungmin Kwon, "Re-worlding Culture?: YouTube as a K-pop interlocutor," in *The Korean Wave: Korean Media Go Global*, ed. Youna Kim (New York: Routledge, 2013), 207.
54 "K-Pop—Topic," *YouTube*, last accessed March 15, 2020, www.youtube.com/channel/UCsEonk9fs_9jmtw9PwER9yg.

Introduction

55 Ono and Kwon, "Re-worlding," 200.
56 Marie-Laure Ryan, "Will New Media Produce New Narratives?," in *Narrative across Media: The Languages of Storytelling*, ed. Marie-Laure Ryan (Lincoln: University of Nebraska Press, 2004), 337.
57 Marie-Laure Ryan and Jan-Noel Thon, "Sotryworlds across Media: Introduction," in *Storyworlds across Media: Toward a Media-Conscious Narratology*, ed. Marie-Laure Ryan and Jan-Noel Thon (Lincoln: University of Nebraska Press, 2014), 2.
58 Marshall McLuhan, *Essential McLuhan*, ed. Eric McLuhan and Frank Zingrone (New York: Basic Books, 1996), 188.
59 Semiotic approach to media is concerned with understanding the narrative power of language, image, sound, movement, face-to-face interaction, as well as the combination of these features of media. A technical approach, on the other hand, investigates broadly how technologies configure the relationship between sender and receiver of media. Lastly, a cultural approach explores behaviors of users and producers of media, as well as the institutions that guarantee the existence of media. For more, see Ryan and Thon, "Storyworlds."
60 James Phelan, *Living To Tell About It* (Ithaca: Cornell University Press, 2005), 5.
61 David Herman, *Story Logic* (Lincoln: University of Nebraska Press, 2002), 9.
62 Ibid.
63 Young Min Baek, "Relationship Between Cultural Distance and Cross-Cultural Distance and Cross-Cultural Music Video Consumption on YouTube," *Social Science Computer Review* 33, no. 6 (2015): 733.
64 See, for instance, Wai-Chung Ho, "Between Globalization and Localization: A Study of Hong Kong Popular Music," *Popular Music* 22, no. 2 (2003): 143–157 and Eun-Young Jung, "Transnational Korea: A Critical Assessment of the Korean Wave in Asia and the United States," *Southeast Review of Asian Studies* 31 (2009): 69–80.
65 Steven Hein, "Cultural Psychology" in *Handbook of Social Psychology*, ed. Susan Fiske, Daniel Gilbert, and Gardner Lindzey (Hoboken, NJ: John Wiley, 2010): 1423.
66 Manuel Castells explains "network society" as a new form of society where the advancement of the electronic media leads to fundamental shifts in society, mobilizing and reorganizing its actors and their activities in a space not of places but of flows. See Eugenia Siapera, *Cultural Diversity and Global Media* (Oxford: Wiley-Blackwell, 2010), 184.
67 Bertha Chin and Lori Hitchcock Morimoto, "Towards a Theory of Transcultural Fandom," *Participations: Journal of Audience & Reception Studies*, 10, no. 1 (2013): 98.
68 James Phelan, *Somebody Telling Somebody Else* (Columbus: Ohio State University, 2017), 5
69 Ibid.

70 Ibid., 7.
71 Toby Miller and Marwan Kraidy, *Global Media Studies* (Cambridge: Polity Press, 2016), 16.
72 David Herman, *Basic Elements of Narrative* (Malden: Wiley-Blackwell, 2009), 106.
73 Ryan, "Story/Worlds/Media," 43.
74 Han Kang's novel was first published in Korean in 2007. Its English translation by Deborah Smith was published in 2015.
75 Ancco's graphic memoir was first published in Korean in 2012. Its English translation by Janet Hong was published in 2016.
76 I use the term in the sense of Russian formalism to mean the process of defamiliarization. For more, see Viktor Shklovsky, *Theory of Prose* (Chicago: Dalkey Archive Press, 1993).
77 Suzanne Keen, "A Theory of Narrative Empathy," *Narrative* 14, no. 3 (2006): 208.
78 Focalization is the perspective or point of view "in terms of which the narrated situations and events are presented; the perceptual or conceptual position in terms of which they are rendered." See Gerald Prince, *Dictionary of Narratology* (Lincoln: University of Nebraska Press, 1989), 31.
79 See Lisa Zunshine, *Getting Inside Your Head: What Cognitive Science Can Tell Us About Popular Culture* (Baltimore: Johns Hopkins University Press, 2012).
80 Ibid., 397.

Bibliography

Baek, Young Min. "Relationship Between Cultural Distance and Cross-Cultural Distance and Cross-Cultural Music Video Consumption on YouTube." *Social Science Computer Review* 33, no. 6 (2015): 730–748.

Burgess, Jean. "YouTube and the Formalization of Amateur Media." In *Amateur Media: Social, Cultural and Legal Perspectives*, edited by Dan Hunter, Ramon Lobato, Julian Thomas, and Megan Richardson, 53–58. London: Routledge, 2013.

Castells, Manuel. *The Rise of the Network Society*. Oxford: Wiley-Blackwell, 2000.

Chang, Kyung-Sup Chang. "Compressed Modernity in South Korea." In *Routledge Handbook of Korean Culture and Society*, edited by Youna Kim, 31–47. New York: Routledge, 2016.

Chaudhary, Vivek Chaudhary. "Feast from the East—Why Britain is Surfing the Korean Culture Wave." *The Guardian*. April 21 (2019). www.theguardian.com/music/2019/apr/21/feast-from-east-britain-surfing-korean-culture-wave.

Chen, Kuan Hsing. *Asia as Method: Toward Deimperialization*. Durham: Duke University Press, 2010.

Chin, Bertha and Lori Hitchcock Morimoto. "Towards a Theory of Transcultural Fandom." *Participations: Journal of Audience & Reception Studies*, 10, no. 1 (2013): 92–108.

Clement, Jessica Clement. "Countries with the Fastest Average Mobile Internet Speeds as of May 2020." *statista*. June 25 (2020). www.statista.com/statistics/896768/countries-fastest-average-mobile-internet-speeds/.

Curan, James and Myung-Jin Park. *De-Westernizing Media Studies*. New York: Routledge, 2000.

Jin, Dal Yong. "How to Understand the Emergence of Digital Korea." In *Routledge Handbook of Korean Culture and Society*, edited by Youna Kim, 179–192. New York: Routledge, 2016.

Dator, Jim and Yongseok Seo. "Korea as the Wave of a Future." *Journal of Future Studies* 9 (2004): 31–44.

Duarte, Fernando. "Which country works the longest hours?" *BBC News*. Last accessed March 8 (2020). www.bbc.com/worklife/article/20180504-which-country-works-the-longest-hours.

Guschwan, Matthew. "New Media: Online Fandom." *Soccer & Society* 17, no. 3 (2016): 351–371.

Hein, Steven. "Cultural Psychology." In *Handbook of Social Psychology*, edited by Susan Fiske, Daniel Gilbert, and Gardner Lindzey. Hoboken, NJ: John Wiley, 2010.

Herman, David. *Story Logic*. Lincoln: University of Nebraska Press, 2002.

———. *Basic Elements of Narrative*. Malden: Wiley-Blackwell, 2009.

Ho, Wai-Chung. "Between Globalization and Localization: A Study of Hong Kong Popular Music." *Popular Music* 22, no. 2 (2003): 143–157.

Hogan, Patrick. *The Mind and Its Stories: Narrative Universals and Human Emotions*. Cambridge: Cambridge University Press, 2003.

———. "Of Literary Universals: Ninety-Five Theses." *Philosophy and Literature* 32, no. 1 (2008): 145–160.

Hyesu, Park. *Media Culture in Transnational Asia: Convergences and Divergences*. New Brunswick: Rutgers University Press, 2020.

"Internet Usage Statistics: The Internet Big Picture." *Internet World Stats*. Last modified March 31, 2019. www.internetworldstats.com/stats.htm.

Ji-young, Sohn. "Korean Market Grows for Online, Mobile Games." *The Korean Herald*. June 20 (2018). www.koreaherald.com/view.php?ud=20180620000648.

Jung, Eun-Young. "Transnational Korea: A Critical Assessment of the Korean Wave in Asia and the United States." *Southeast Review of Asian Studies* 31 (2009): 69–80.

Kang, Jiyeon. "Coming to Terms with 'Unreasonable' Global Power: The 2002 South Korean Candlelight Vigils." *Communication and Critical/Cultural Studies* 6, no. 2 (2009): 171–192.

Keen, Suzanne. "A Theory of Narrative Empathy." *Narrative* 14, no. 3 (2006): 207–236.

Kim, Youna. "Korean Wave Pop Culture in the Global Internet Age: Why Poplar? Why Now?" In *The Korean Wave: Korean Media Go Global*, edited by Youna Kim, 75–92. New York: Routledge, 2013.

———. "Introduction: Korean Media in a Digital Cosmopolitan World." In *The Korean Wave: Korean Media Go Global*, edited by Youna Kim, 1–27.

New York: Routledge, 2013. "K-Pop—Topic." *YouTube*. Last accessed March 15, 2020. www.youtube.com/channel/UCsEonk9fs_9jmtw9PwER9yg.
Lee, Sanghoon and Jae-Il Jung. "Telecommunications Markets, Industry, and Infrastructure in Korea." *IEEE Communications Magazine* 36 (1998): 59–64.
Lee, Dong-Hoo. "Digital Cameras, Personal Photography and the Reconfiguration of Spatial Experiences." *The Information Society* 26 (2010): 266–275.
Lim, Sun Sun and Cheryll Ruth R. Soriano. "A (Digital) Giant Awakens—Invigorating Media Studies with Asian Perspectives." In *Asian Perspectives on Digital Culture*, edited by Sun Sun Lim and Cheryll Ruth R. Soriano, 3–14. New York: Routledge, 2016.
Liu, Marian. "Beyond Beauty: Korean Makeup Provides 'Cosmeceuticals.'" *CNN*. April 11 (2018). www.cnn.com/2018/04/11/health/korean-makeup-beauty-health-benefits/index.html.
McLuhan, Marshall. *Essential McLuhan*, edited by Eric McLuhan and Frank Zingrone. New York: Basic Books, 1996.
Miller, Toby and Marwan Kraidy. *Global Media Studies*. Cambridge: Polity Press, 2016.
Mingas, Melanie. "South Korea Leads 5G Deployment." *Capacity*. February 27 (2020). www.capacitymedia.com/articles/3824986/south-korea-leads-5g-deployment.
O'Dea, S. "Smartphone Ownership Rate by Country 2018." *Statista*. February 27 (2020). www.statista.com/statistics/539395/smartphone-penetration-worldwide-by-country/.
Ono, Kent A. and Jungmin Kwon. "Re-worlding Culture?: YouTube as a K-pop Interlocutor." In *The Korean Wave: Korean Media Go Global*, edited by Youna Kim, 199–214. New York: Routledge, 2013.
Phelan, James. *Living to Tell About It*. Ithaca: Cornell University Press, 2005.
_____. *Somebody Telling Somebody Else*. Columbus: Ohio State University, 2017.
Prince, Gerald. *Dictionary of Narratology*. Lincoln: University of Nebraska Press, 1989.
Ryan, Marie-Laure. "Story/Worlds/Media: Tuning the Instruments of a Media-Conscious Narratology." In *Storyworlds across Media: Towards a Media-Conscious Narratology*, edited by Marie-Laure Ryan and Jan-Noël Thon, 25–49. Lincoln: University of Nebraska Press, 2014.
_____. "Will New Media Produce New Narratives?" In *Narrative across Media: The Languages of Storytelling*, edited by Marie-Laure Ryan, 337–359. Lincoln: University of Nebraska Press, 2004.
Ryan, Marie-Laure and Jan-Noel Thon. "Storyworlds across Media: Introduction." In *Storyworlds across Media: Toward a Media-Conscious Narratology*, edited by Marie-Laure Ryan and Jan-Noel Thon, 1–21. Lincoln: University of Nebraska Press, 2014.
Shklovsky, Viktor. *Theory of Prose*. Chicago: Dalkey Archive Press, 1993.
Siapera, Eugenia. *Cultural Diversity and Global Media*. Oxford: Wiley-Blackwell, 2010.

So, Won. "Enrollment Rate in University in South Korea from 2009 to 2019." *statista*. June 22 (2020). www.statista.com/statistics/629032/south-korea-university-enrollment-rate/.

"South Korea GDP per capita PPP." *Trading Economics*. Last accessed May 5, 2020. https://tradingeconomics.com/south-korea/gdp-per-capita-ppp.

"South Korea Has the Lowest Overweight among all the OECD Nations, but!" (my trans.). *Joongang Ilbo* online. Last modified January 23 (2015). https://news.joins.com/article/17010069.

"Top-15 Semiconductor Suppliers 2018." *Anysilicon*. August 20 (2018). https://anysilicon.com/top-15-semiconductor-suppliers-2018/.

Wai Sim Lau, Dorothy. "Star Construction in the Era of Media Convergence." In *Media Culture in Transnational Asia: Convergences and Divergences*, edited by Hyesu Park, 54–71. New Brunswick: Rutgers University Press, 2020.

Wandering Shadow. "The "BTS Effect" on South Korea's Economy, Industry and Culture." *Medium*. May 30 (2019). https://medium.com/@shadow_twts/the-bts-effect-on-south-koreas-economy-industry-and-culture-975e8933da56.

Wang, Amy X. "How K-Pop Conquered the West." *RollingStone*. August 21 (2018). www.rollingstone.com/music/music-features/bts-kpop-albums-bands-global-takeover-707139/.

Zunshine, Lisa. *Getting Inside Your Head: What Cognitive Science Can Tell Us about Popular Culture*. Baltimore: Johns Hopkins University Press, 2012.

1 Korean literature wave

Transcultural and transnational reading of *The Vegetarian* and *Bad Friend*

This chapter examines contemporary South Korean (hereafter Korean) literature in English translation, using Han Kang's novel *The Vegetarian*[1] and Ancco's graphic memoir *Bad Friend*[2] as case studies. While much attention has been paid to Korean popular songs (K-pop), films, and televisual dramas (K-drama) as important contributors to the worldwide spread of Korean popular culture, much less ink has been spilled on Korean literature and its reception globally. This may be due to several reasons. First, literature, which primarily relies on the traditional print media platform, cannot be circulated as readily and quickly as audio-visual cultural artifacts, such as K-pop and K-drama, which can be digitized and uploaded to the Internet and shared by a wide range of audiences at any time and place (and often at no cost). Second, the publishing industry in South Korea has been stagnating domestically with less and less people reading books. According to a study conducted by the Ministry of Sports, Culture, and Tourism, 59.9 percent of adults and 91.7 percent of students responded that they read one book or less during a one-year period from October 2016 to September 2017 (excluding comics, magazines, textbooks, and educational texts). The decline in reading habits is gradual and evident, as the percentages in 2016–2017 dropped by 5.4 percentage points among adults and 3.2 among students compared to the same study done in 2015.[3]

The last reason, which I plan to dwell on more in my discussion of *The Vegetarian*, has to do with the complex issues of translation. Korean literature, except for few rare cases, such as Shin Kyung-sook's *Please Look After Mom*[4] and Hwang Sun-mi's children's book *The Hen Who Dreamed She Could Fly*,[5] "remains unappealing and peripheral at best to American readers."[6] Hwang Sok-young, one of the most eminent South Korean contemporary writers, notes this apparent invisibility of Korean literature in the global market and says that the biggest challenge in the globalization of Korean literature is "the lack of skilled translators who can properly translate Korean literary works into English."[7] Likewise, Kim San-in, president of the Literature Translation Institute of Korea, the state-funded institute whose mission is "to globalize Korean literature through systematized translation and networking," echoes Hwang's concern:

> The overall problem … is the lack of translators. … There are not many literary translators who could be given a project with full trust. The situation with English might be better, but for other languages, there are not many choices.[8]

In the rest of the chapter, I examine *The Vegetarian* and *Bad Friend* as the two success cases of the globalization of Korean literature. Through close reading of the two literary texts in English translation, I aim to show elements of their narratives that may have contributed to their popular receptions globally. *The Vegetarian*, for instance, is aesthetically (aesthetic uncanny and striking visual elements), formally (three-part construction with diverse perspectives), and narratologically (use of unnatural narrative and feminist narratology) rich in its construction. Additionally, the novel is thematically timely and universal (ecofeminism, among other things, for instance) while contextually specific simultaneously (set in contemporary South Korea and situated within Korea's patriarchal family dynamics). The consequence is the compelling weaving together of the universal and the particular, which helps to enstrange[9] global readers effectively and renew their perspectives. *Bad Friend*, on the other hand, uses a medium that is relatively freer from the obstacle of translation, that is, graphic narrative, and relies on both the visual and verbal narratives to communicate to readers. *Bad Friend*, in particular, capitalizes on the graphic medium in order to illustrate what is universally unspeakable, repulsive, and distressing: the life of an adolescent growing up with sexual abuse, teen prostitution, violence, and drugs. Whereas "novel reading can be so easily stopped or interrupted by unpleasant emotional reaction to a book,"[10] Ancco's careful visual choices, use of the first-person autobiographical narration and focalization,[11] and the overall lyric quality of the narrative as a dominant mode of progression, enhance readers' affective engagement with the narrative. Importantly, too, these authorial decisions, as my analysis of the memoir will show, establish a push-pull effect between readers and the narrative and enable readers to bear witness to painful memories illustrated by the author.

The Vegetarian: eco-feminism, unnatural narrative, and unreadable mind

In its original Korean version, published in 2007, *The Vegetarian* starts with a passage that can be translated thus: "Before my wife turned vegetarian, I'd never thought of anything particular about her."[12] This same opening line, however, sounds quite different in Deborah Smith's 2015 English translation: "Before my wife turned vegetarian, I'd always thought of her as completely unremarkable in every way."[13] In the original Korean version, the narrator of Part I of the novel, protagonist Yeong-hye's husband Mr. Cheong, sounds simply dull, accustomed or indifferent at best. By contrast, Smith's translation is likely to provoke in the minds of readers strongly negative responses toward the narrator; he is demeaning, condescending, and overly judgmental. It is hence not surprising that Smith's translation of *The Vegetarian* raised doubts and criticism among literary scholars and translators in Korea despite the fact that Kang and Smith together won the Man Booker International prize in 2016 for the English translation.[14] Charse Yun, fluent in both Korean and English, for instance, points out that "10.9% of the first part of the novel was mistranslated. Another 5.7% of the original text was omitted. And this was just the first section."[15] While mistranslation occurs even in the best of translations, what may be most disturbing are the stylistic differences that Smith made to the novel through her translation: "I find it hard to come up with an adequate analogy, but imagine the plain, contemporary style of Raymond Carver being garnished with the elaborate diction of Charles Dickens."[16]

Yun's concern is not exaggerated, as Smith herself acknowledged: "Translating from Korean into English involves moving from a language more accommodating of ambiguity, repetition, and plain prose, to one that favours precision, concision, and lyricism."[17] The controversy surrounding Smith's translation of Kang's novel invites deeper considerations for the political implications involved in the process of translation. After all, there is a clear relation between language and politics/power, as seen in many cases of language conversion in the colonized by the colonizer; and translation, the act of converting from one language to the other, is never free from the political and cultural elements and implications of the new language. Many scholars of translation studies have thus paid close attention to this implicit political and cultural power of translation, calling translation an act of manipulation[18] and "a process of gathering and creating *new information* that can be turned to powerful political ends."[19] In this context, Smith's subjugating the unique styles and characteristics of the Korean language to those of the dominant language, English, is indeed troubling to say the least, as it ends up obscuring and further undermining the original (Korean) voice. Nevertheless, Smith's voice added to the novel has made *The Vegetarian* "the biggest 'win'" in Korean translated literature since Shin Kyung-Sook's *Please Look After Mom* won the Man Asian Literary Prize in 2012.[20] Domestic sales of the novel also increased drastically after the prize. The novel maintained its best-seller status for three weeks in 2016, nine years after it was first published in Korea. If, as mentioned earlier, the overall problem of the peripheral position of Korean literature in the global market is the lack of translators, Deborah Smith's emergence in Korean translated literature is still a welcoming scene even when the political, cultural, and linguistic implications of the act of translation should further be considered carefully.[21]

What translation cannot easily manipulate, however, are the structural, formal, and narratological choices that the author makes in the construction of his/her original narrative. Translating the third-person narration in the original text into the first-person narration, for instance, will simply be unthinkable. Therefore, my focus in the discussion of *The Vegetarian* is on some of these important narratological and formal choices that Han Kang has made in her novel and how these choices inform reading of the novel within and across geographic borders. Many scholars and reviewers of *The Vegetarian* have approached the novel with a feminist perspective. They note that the novel represents women and their oppression in a patriarchal society. As Yeong-hye defies the dominant social norms (carnivore-oriented diet, womanly beauty, womanly submission), Yeong-hye is oppressed and violated by her own family and society at large. Rincy Chandran and Geetha Pai, for instance, adopting an eco-feminist framework, interpret the carnivore diet, which Yeong-hye refuses to comply with, as a form of domination and violence and believe that "[o]pression of the nature and of women by patriarchy must be examined together."[22] Paola Bica, on the other hand, turns to postmodern poetics and posits that since "there are multiple realities and everything can be questioned [within the postmodern framework]," Yeong-hye's marginalized position in society invites postmodernist re-reading of female subjectivity and renews our understanding of the relation between individual and society.[23]

Although these perspectives are illuminating, I am more interested in the ways in which Han Kang responds to and further complicates such universal and timely thematic concerns through her specific authorial choices and by situating the novel in a uniquely Korean context. The effect is two-fold. On the one hand, Kang's formal choices significantly shape readers' cognitive and affective responses to the novel in such a way that they move beyond their differing cultural and national backgrounds and step into the position of Kang's authorial audience.[24] On the other hand, the novel's Korean context invites reconsideration for Western theoretical frameworks (eco-feminism and postmodernism, for instance) and how South Korean writers are actively participating in the new dynamics of globalization, which, according to Roland Robertson, can be formulated as "a massive, two-fold process involving the interpenetration of the universalization of particularism and the particularization of universalism."[25] In the rest of my discussion, I will demonstrate how this "new dynamics of globalization" unfolds in *The Vegetarian*. I will also pay particular attention to Han Kang's narratological and formal innovations, including the compelling ways in which Han Kang constructs Yeong-hye's unreadable fictional mind and uses her inscrutability as a powerful rhetorical tool to engage readers cognitively, affectively, and ethically.

Part I of the novel is narrated and focalized by Yeong-hye's husband, Mr. Cheong, who finds Yeong-hye and her vegetarianism impenetrable, disturbing, and unacceptable. This sentiment is shared by many other characters in the novel. The wife of Mr. Cheong's boss, for instance, comments on Yeong-hye's vegetarianism at a dinner gathering: "It seems to me that one shouldn't be too narrow-minded when it comes to food."[26] Yeong-hye's refusal to eat meat, moreover, makes her inscrutable: "Was it possible that she hadn't grasped the status of the elegant middle-aged woman facing her? What shadowy recesses lurked in her mind, what secrets I'd never suspected? In that moment, she was utterly unknowable."[27] Mr. Cheong's attempt to find an "acceptable" reason for Yeong-hye's vegetarianism meets no success, as her only answer is, "I had a dream." Yeong-hye's inscrutability has notable thematic and interpretive consequences. For instance, Porter Abbott, in "Unreadable Minds and the Captive Reader," outlines three types of default reading positions in fiction made possible through unreadable minds. Namely, characters who appear to be unreadable can be stereotyped by others, invite a symbolic reading, or operate in the characterization of another as "a catalyst in a drama of non-reading, with the focus on the captive reader as she/he copes with the unreadable."[28] Likewise, and as many other reviewers and scholars of the novel have noticed already, Yeong-hye's unreadability can be interpreted symbolically and invite eco-feminist readings of the novel where the oppression and marginalization She experiences by the dominant majority (that is, those who do eat meat) equate to the oppression of nature.

Meanwhile, by focusing on Mr. Cheong's perspective and how he confronts Yeong-hye's unreadability, Part I of the novel also shows clearly how he fails to evolve into the "captive reader." Mr. Cheong chooses to marginalize and undermine Yeong-hye's subjectivity rather than to cope with her and becoming a captive reader of her unreadable mind. For Yeong-hye's unreadable mind to work as "a catalyst in a drama of non-reading," then, Han Kang's readers, by engaging deeply with Yeong-hye's inscrutability, must step into the narrative and assume the role of the captive reader who is absent in the novel. Of course, to do so may pose certain challenges to readers. As Brian McHale, in his discussion of postmodern literature argues, "since the reader's involvement in the fictional world is normally channeled through its characters, the cancelation or de-creation of a character has particularly disorienting consequences."[29] The cancelation of Yeong-hye's character—that is, her being rendered unreadable and inaccessible by other characters in the novel—is, however, more empowering than disorienting. As my analysis of the novel will show, through her impenetrability, Yeong-hye rejects any objectification of her mind and body, which allows for the construction of multiple narratives and storyworlds[30] against the dominant narrative (the one narrated by Mr. Cheong) and invites multiple narratee and reader positions (the one addressed by Mr. Cheong on the one hand and the other addressed by Yeong-hye on the other). The consequence is that readers engage with the novel in such a way that they actively move through multiple layers of narrative in their attempt to create meaning for Yeong-hye. Yeong-hye's unknowability in the novel becomes, in other words, the very "catalyst" for readers who participate in "a drama of non-reading" as the very "captive reader."

In order to achieve these effects, Han Kang inserts dream-like sequences narrated by Yeong-hye. Because Yeong-hye's narration takes the form of an extended interior monologue, however, no one in the novel has access to her interiority:

> But the fear. My clothes still wet with blood. ... My bloody hands. My bloody mouth. In that barn, what had I done? Pushed that red raw mass into my mouth, felt it squish against my gum, the roof of my mouth, slick with crimson blood.[31]

While Yeong-hye is only externally focalized[32] by Mr. Cheong, who finds her unreadable, these interior monologues internally focalize[33] Yeong-hye's consciousness for readers. These secretive, private disclosures to readers of Yeong-hye's interiority make clear how she equates meat-eating with human violence and oppression, and how she considers herself to be a participant in this violence. By refusing to partake in meat-eating, however, Yeong-hye ends up subjecting herself to the very same violence and oppression in return. In another moment of interior monologue, Yeong-hye's voice becomes even stronger: "*One time, just one more time, I want to shout. I want to throw myself through the pitch-black window. ... Nobody can help me. Nobody can save me. Nobody can make me breathe.*"[34]

Although Yeong-hye is consistently self-destructive, her voice in these narrative moments is simultaneously assertive and strong-willed. Likewise, the repetition of the first-person "I" and negation ("Nobody") enables Yeong-hye to exercise her agency and voice, to indicate her independent will, and to refuse any external force to be imposed upon her. Moreover, Yeong-hye's interior monologues lead to constituting a "private text" within the novel, an embedded subtext that offers an alternate reading of a character or events—a story within a story that often reveals something that is crucial, deep, and secretive at the heart of the narrative.[35] Yeong-hye's private text draws attention to the constructed nature of Han Kang's narrative and challenges the dominant patriarchal ideology, as the version of Yeong-hye emerging from her interior monologues, the private text, makes a stark contrast with, and powerfully subverts, that of the voiceless, inscrutable Yeong-hye as externally depicted by Mr. Cheong. It also helps realize the presence of multiple voices and carriers of these voices in the novel, invoking multiple narratee positions,[36] which readers may occupy, although "the degree to which [the reader] can also feel addressed can vary from narrative to narrative."[37] Yeong-hye's embedded voice with its exclusive nature, however, strongly increases the degree "to which [Kang's readers] can also feel addressed." After all, no one in the novel is able or willing to listen to Yeong-hye, while readers alone are allowed exclusive access to her interiority. As a result, readers more willingly join Yeong-hye's private discourse as her empathetic confidants.

Readers' empathetic identification with Yeong-hye is likely to increase toward the end of Part I. Yeong-hye's entire family gathers for a family meal at In-hye's, Yeong-hye's younger sister. Yeong-hye's patriarchal, hot-tempered father is determined to change her decision to be a vegetarian, as Mr. Cheong describes it: "'My heart will pack in if this goes on any longer!' my father-in-law shouted at Yeong-hye. 'Don't you understand what your father's telling you? If he tells you to eat, you eat!'"[38] As Yeong-hye continues to refuse to eat any meat, the gathering takes a traumatically violent turn:

> Having thrown down the chopstick, [my father-in-law] now picked up a piece of pork with his fingers and approached my wife. ... 'Father, I beg you, stop this,' In-hye entreated him, but he shook her

off and thrust the pork at my wife's lips. A moaning sound came from her tightly closed mouth. She was unable to say even a single word in case, when she opened her mouth to speak, the meat found its way in.[39]

As soon as Yeong-hye is released from her father, she picks up a fruit knife and slashes her wrist then falls unconscious and is taken to a hospital.

The scene depicts male dominance over the female body and consciousness literally. Yeong-hye is forcefully held down by her hot-tempered father, while her husband merely observes the escalation of the violence. Yeong-hye's own violent response, of course, is self-destructive and abusive, but is also a powerful expression of her will to challenge the patriarchy and its domination—a point that readers, once joining the position of Yeong-hye's empathetic narratee, appreciate and may even embrace. Moreover, while foregrounding the binary power structure between male and female and thereby inviting feminist reading of the situation, the scene simultaneously adds a layer that is culturally unique to Korea (and Asia more generally) where, according to the Confucian virtue, "a woman is required to obey to her father, husband, and son"[40] and eating is considered to be a communal and familial ceremony. Regular Korean meals are comprised of "bowls of rice [that are] served individually, but *banchan*, or side dishes, and *jjigae*, or stew, are often served communally, meant to be shared."[41] In this particular Korean context, then, family members are expected to share similar eating habits and preferences. Hence, Yeong-hye's decision to be a vegetarian and thereby not share common eating habits with her family prompts her father to challenge her both physically and emotionally. Seen this way, the scene particularizes a general feminist reading of the novel within the specific Korean cultural context and captures conflicts between the feminist value of independence and self-expression on the one hand and the Confucian value of communalism and family identity on the other.

These cultural references help form and distinctly impact the novel's multiple implied readers. Implied reader, according to Wolfgang Iser, "incorporates both the prestructuring of the potential meaning of the text, and the reader's actualization of this potential through the reading process."[42] Implied reader, in other words, is a textual concept incorporated in the text and to whom the author addresses his narrative—it is a position that the author's reader through his/her reading process steps into in order to make sense of the narrative. Brian Richardson, in "Singular Text, Multiple Implied Readers," further pushes the concept of implied reader and explores "the possibilities of multiple implied readers inscribed within the same text."[43] The formation of multiple implied readers is frequently evident in narratives written by writers from former colonies who, in a dialectic "informed by concepts of authenticity, universality, local respect, and international sales," wish to write for an indigenous audience, but do not wish to needlessly alienate "the larger Anglo-, Franco-, or Lusophone world."[44] The subsequent consequence is the tension between the universal and the particular, which, in the case of literature, often leads to a source of creative possibilities.

Indeed, the family scene of the novel is likely to elicit multiple responses and evaluations from multiple implied readers of the novel. Those readers who are more familiar with the Confucian, communal value of family and family meals may find the scene highly mimetic and appreciate the ways in which the author deepens feminist reading of the novel through a culturally particularized reading. By contrast, those readers who are unfamiliar with such cultural references could regard the scene, while thematically powerful with its strong feminist resonance, as overly dramatized, emotional, and even contrived.[45] The point is not necessarily that one group of readers (the one that can contextualize the scene culturally) is superior to the other (the one that does not contextualize), although Richardson notes that it is evident that "there is often a distinct hierarchy among these readers [prestructured in the same text], and that it is an epistemological one: one reader knows both what the other perceives and what it alone can know."[46] What is more important is to recognize is how rich and complex the scene becomes when considering more deeply the author's careful orchestration of narrative and culture, as well as how this orchestration influences readers' reading experience in specifically guided ways.

Yeong-hye's divergence from the expected social and cultural norms renders her not only inscrutable, but also unnatural. For instance, Mr. Cheong's boss's wife comments that "[m]eat eating is a fundamental human instinct, which means vegetarianism goes against human nature, right? It just isn't natural."[47] The unnatural in narratives, or the examination of unnatural phenomena in narratives, has been the focus of study among theorists of unnatural narratology. The unnatural as conceptualized by these scholars, however, is primarily concerned with conventional and generic impossibilities of narrative,[48] or physical and logical impossibilities—for instance, how textual reality of a given narrative defies the logic and physics of the extra-textual reality.[49] The unnatural in *The Vegetarian* adds another layer to the existing theory of unnatural by highlighting how customs and rules of the extra-textual reality may determine what human behaviors and emotions can be accepted in fiction as natural, and what can be denied as unnatural. Under the generalizing and often oppressive structure and rules of society and culture, individuals who resist conventions of the majority can be ostracized and considered abnormal and unnatural, just as Yeong-hye is in *The Vegetarian*.

Yeong-hye's unnaturalness also takes various forms, depending on the perspective of who is judging her. Mr. Cheong equates Yeong-hye's unnaturalness to the non-human, as his description of her at the family meal scene suggests: "As soon as the strength in Yeong-ho's arms was visibly exhausted, my wife growled and spat out the meat. An animal cry of distress burst from her lips."[50] Yeong-hye's brother-in-law, a failing artist, who develops a voyeuristic fetish for Yeong-hye's body and paints flowers on her naked body, sexualizes Yeong-hye (he later forces himself upon her):[51]

> A thrilling energy seemed to flow out quietly from some unknowable place inside his body and collect on the tip of his brush. ... [S]he looked as if she were sleeping ... Her calm acceptance of all these things made her seem to him something sacred. Whether human, animal or plant, she could not be called a "person," but then she wasn't exactly some feral creature either—more like a mysterious being with qualities of both.[52]

Her brother-in-law's voyeuristic perspective objectifies and sexualizes Yeong-hye as "a mysterious being" whose subjectivity is erased and who, while accepting all, cannot be called a "person" at all. The unnaturalization of Yeong-hye's character by these male characters and their perspectives may well indicate, as Bica in her essay points out, that Han Kang subverts character hierarchy: "the protagonist does not have a predominant voice, she is the object of perspective of other people, and she is presented as insubstantial with a lack of action and identity."[53]

Bica's reading of the subverted character hierarchy is limiting, however, as it focuses solely on the primary level of narrative—the level of narrative constructed by the voices and perspectives of Mr. Cheong and Yeong-hye's brother in law. This view may well change if one looks into the embedded narrative within the primary narrative. As pointed out earlier, although Yeong-hye is inscrutable, "unnatural," and the very victim of patriarchal domination, Yeong-hye becomes the narrator and central force of the narrative in her private text, revealing her interiority and actively reaching out to her narratee. Moreover, precisely because no other character in the novel can access Yeong-hye's consciousness, readers are given the powerful role of her sole listener. Yeong-hye's active telling and readers' empathetic listening together allow her to establish and exercise her own substantial agency and the very "predominant voice." This extra layer of narrative space that Yeong-hye and readers co-create is a meaningful interpretive zone within which the new dynamics for narrative and character hierarchy can be realized.

As the novel progresses toward Part 3, titled "Flaming Trees," narrated by a third-person narrator, and focalized by In-hye, social and cultural restraints on Yeong-hye lead her to embark on the process of turning into a tree:

> Look sister, I'm doing a handstand, leaves are growing out of my body, roots are sprouting out of my hands ... they delve down into the earth. Endlessly, endlessly ... yes, I spread my legs because I wanted flowers to bloom from my crotch, I spread them wide.[54]

Yeong-hye's metamorphosis to a tree seems to suggest that she "creates an in-between state of mind in which she is looking for her liberation and independence but still suffering from social oppression."[55] Through this metamorphosis, Yeong-hye clearly moves beyond the boundary of what is humanly natural and possible, but readers, with their privileged access to her perspective, are able to make sense of this unnaturalness. For Yeong-hye, being normal and acceptable in her most "natural" human form means rendering herself both the object of, and cause for, oppression and violence, as she discloses through her interior monologue earlier in the novel: "*Can only trust my breasts now. I like my breasts, nothing can be killed by them. Hand, foot, tongue, gaze, all weapons from which nothing is safe. But not my breasts.*"[56] Yeong-hye's attempt to abandon her human form and become a tree can be interpreted as an act of resistance and independence. This attempt, however, is neither successful nor complete. Yeong-hye, as her own description of the transformation indicates, is neither a human nor a tree and is rather stuck in-between. Even In-hye, who is equally oppressed and is most empathetic toward Yeong-hye, fails to fully share her sister's perspective: "I have dreams too, you know. Dreams ... and I could let myself dissolve into them ... but surely the dream isn't all there is? We have to wake up at some point, don't we?"[57]

The novel, while suggesting Yeong-hye's gradual demise, ends with internal focalization of In-hye: "In-hye stares fiercely at the trees. As if waiting for an answer. As if protesting against something. The look in her eyes is dark and insistent."[58] Has In-hye embraced Yeong-hye's metamorphosis and its implications? In-hye's fierce look at the trees may signal that she has finally stepped into Yeong-hye's perspective. Nevertheless, In-hye is still unsure and protesting against the unknown. While her look is fierce, it is simultaneously "dark." The ambiguity of In-hye's vantage point does not offer a clear answer about how to interpret Yeong-hye's last act. While it is empowering, it is self-destructive, and even In-hye, who gets closest to Yeong-hye's mind in the novel, fails to fully identify with it. This ambiguous ending of the novel without complete closure is, however, powerful. After all, In-hye has not stopped questioning Yeong-hye's struggle, as she is still "waiting for an answer" with eyes that are "insistent." This insistence, perhaps, is the gesture that will resonate in the minds of Han Kang's readers well beyond the last page of the novel.

In *The Vegetarian* Han Kang constructs a narrative that is rich in theme (feminism and postmodernism in their intersections with Korean cultural specificities) and innovative in its shape (multiple narrative layers and perspectives that impact the reader's positionality). While readers, regardless of their cultural backgrounds, are offered narrative tools that allow them to come to identify with Yeong-hye's struggle (an exclusive access to her interiority through her private text embedded within the primary narrative), readers, depending on their cultural backgrounds, may differently interpret and evaluate specific instances of the novel. The resulting effect is a dynamic narrative text that simultaneously is uniquely Korean and universally global. We may find the key to the national and international success of *The Vegetarian* in this very particularization of the universal and the universalization of the particular.

The rest of the chapter continues to explore the globalization of Korean literature by examining a graphic memoir in English translation, *Bad Friend*.

Bad Friend: visual invitation to painful memories

Ancco's *Bad Friend,* first published in Korean in 2012, has been translated into French, Italian, and English and received numerous prestigious awards abroad, most notably, the New Writer Award at Angoulême International Comics Festival in 2017, the oldest international comics festival, which is held in Angoulême, France. *Bad Friend* is a graphic memoir that tells a story of Jinju, narrator and stand-in for the author, growing up as a rebellious teenager in South Korea during the 1990s. While the memoir follows the typical trajectory of a coming-of-age story, Jinju's life as recalled and illustrated by the present-day Jinju, a comics artist herself, centers on what most readers would probably rather not talk and read about: teen prostitution, sexual abuse, and domestic violence. The memoir's focus on difficult subject matter vis-à-vis the comics medium invites readers to consider a visual narrative's tellability and how comics artists use this narrative form to transmit traumatic memories to readers. And, furthermore, how does the visual narrative medium help engage readers in such a way that they move beyond the role of passive spectators without being too distressed by the negative and unpleasant feelings that such painful memories may provoke in their minds? This question is especially pertinent given that, as Suzanne Keen points out in "A Theory of Narrative Empathy," a "novel [or any form of narrative] reading can be so easily stopped or interrupted by an unpleasant reaction to a book."[59]

In my discussion of *Bad Friend*, I analyze Ancco's visual techniques and how her conscious visual choices shape readers' cognitive, emotional, and ethical responses to the protagonist's experience as retold in the comics medium. I also question, as I did with my analysis of *The Vegetarian*, use of cultural references in the graphic memoir and what impact they may have on readers of diverse national and cultural backgrounds. Numerous studies have been done to examine the use of visual narrative and its power to capture the complexities and subtleties of personal and cultural traumas: Marianne Hirsch's work on Holocaust survivors and what she calls "postmemory,"[60] Judith Butler's study of Susan Sontag's approach to photographic depictions of the suffering of others,[61] and Hillary Chute's work on Art Spiegleman's graphic memoir *Maus*,[62] to name but a few. These and other scholars' approaches to visual narrative raise some important questions to examine, which are echoed in Gillian Whitlock's study of what she calls "autographics." Whitlock asks, "How can we do more than consume these images as passive spectators? How can we move on to recognize the norms that govern which lives will be regarded as human, and the frames through which discourse and visual representation proceed?"[63]

Questions concerning how readers of graphic narrative consume images, and what readerly position they come to take on are especially worth considering since the graphic narrative is a form that capitalizes on "gutters," the empty space between comics frames in which readers must actively participate to bring "closure" and "fil[l] in ... with 'missing' action."[64] The very nature of graphic narrative with gutters implies that the mode of reading in comics ideally becomes more active and participatory. The active readerly participation could, however, be counterproductive when readers are presented with characters whose situations and experiences are so negative and repulsive that engaging too actively and deeply with them could in fact lead not to empathy, but to "personal distress"—an aversive emotional response "characterized by apprehension of another's emotion," causing "turning away from the provocative condition of the other."[65] In Ancco's representation of her characters, then, she has a challenging task at hand—to redress "overdetermined narratives of marginalized subjectivities"[66] by engaging and disengaging readers at the same time. This simultaneous engagement and disengagement is crucial to helping readers remain empathetic while avoiding identifying too closely with characters and their circumstances; and to encouraging readers to step into the fictional world while making sure that readers do not become so distressed by the narrative that they ultimately turn away from it all together.

One way to address this challenge may be using concepts such as focalization, that is, perspective or point of view. Through focalization, readers can learn about character traits, motives, and circumstances and determine whether and how to identify or de-identify with the character. The concept of focalization first appeared in Gerald Genette's influential *Narrative Discourse*, published in 1979. Since then, the term has been revisited and led to many variations and specifications (internal versus external focalization, for instance),[67] but the initial use of the concept was mostly limited to literary narratives that almost always have both the narrator and the character (or a narrator who is also a character), making the investigation of who *tells* versus who *sees* relatively more intuitive. Visual narratives, such as film and comics, require a different approach, however, to voice (who narrates the narrative?) and to point of view (whose perception do we follow?), because these concepts in visual narratives are not as clearly marked as those in literary narratives. In graphic narratives, for instance, the story is told primarily through images in their relation to text in the forms of word balloons (representation of sound/speech), thought balloons (representation of thought), or captions. Captions, boxed or free-standing text that appears inside the panel, can function as commentaries for actions and events in the panel space and are used most frequently in graphic memoirs. Similarly, focalization in graphic narrative "is of a visual nature," as thoughts and perceptions of characters in this narrative form are more often visualized than narrated or talked about.[68] Many different visual techniques can be deployed to capture focalizing character's visual field in graphic narratives: "seeing the shadow of the viewer, the exaggeration of a foregrounded object such as a key hole," or "an image of the character looking at something and then the image of the object looked at."[69]

Likewise, Ancco uses various visual techniques at her disposal—charcoal-soaked panels and specific positioning of characters, for instance—in order to visualize thoughts and feelings of her characters in her graphic memoir. Moreover, Ancco's use of visual focalization is to influence readers' relation to her characters and their points of view, as well as the perceptual position that readers come to occupy—a position that ultimately determines readers' ethical responses to actions and events in the storyworld. This is evident from the very opening page of the memoir. The present-day Jinju is seen from a distant side angle as she lights her cigarette on a small and worn-out balcony. While there is no verbal narrative that indicates clearly what Jinju is thinking and feeling and who is seeing Junju, the charcoal-soaked page adds silence, stasis, and bleakness to the single panel. The same dark and sultry art style continues in the following pages. Now Jinju's figure is more foregrounded, as readers are offered a closer shot of Jinju seated alone on her balcony. As Jinju looks down into the darkness without any movement, her narration, the free-standing caption inside the panel, emerges: "There is no longer a distinction between days and nights any more. It has become a habit for me to look down into the darkness from my balcony."[70] The second panel of the page now focuses on an empty street seen from the balcony, and part of Jinju's hand with a cigarette appearing at the right bottom side of the panel signals that it is Jinju's perspective through which readers are invited into the same darkness and silence. As readers follow Jinju's vantage point, and as Jinju is squarely situated within her balcony (with a dark and narrow alley behind her, and the second balcony overhead boxing her in), readers, too, are positioned within this narrowly depicted zone of heavily weighted bleakness. The spatial make-up of the panel, in other words, illustrates Jinji's perspective and affects readers' perceptual positioning and emotional engagement with Jinju effectively.

Although Jinju's narration inside the panel only plainly describes the dark alley of her neighborhood in the middle of the night, and she, the focalizing character, is seen from the outside without any attempt at narrating or verbalizing her visual field: the use of darkness and specific positioning of Jinju translate the overall mood of stasis and darkness into the minds of readers. This visualization of static mood and use of Jinju's vantage point as the visual focalization seem to gesture that readers share and adopt her perspective, thereby identifying with her. Interestingly, however, Jinju's face—drawn in a sketchy cartoony style— is never fully exposed to readers. They see Jinju either from her side, from a distance, or from behind. Note, also, that it is the visualization of the part of her body, her hand, that helps indicate whose visual field it is that readers are expected to follow. It is almost as though the author refuses to provide fuller disclosure of Jinju's face and mind even while inviting readers to look into the same darkness with her. Consequently, readers concurrently feel closer to, and are distanced from, Jinju. This initial positioning of readers and visualization of Jinju's body and face contribute to the push-pull effect between readers and Jinju, which is crucial to the audience's reading of many pages of the memoir to come. For instance, shortly after this opening scene the memoir turns to the past. Jinju as a teenager smokes, drinks, and spends nights out on streets, and her father becomes more and more abusive in the face of Jinju's rebellion. Readers see a panel of Jinju on the ground and underneath her father, who is relentlessly beating her. On the next page, a series of panels follows—Jinju is hardly visible, and consecutive panels capture her father's hand holding a badminton racket. The page ends with Jinju being left alone in a dark room. She is seated in a crouched position, and her face is completely buried in her arms.

As is true in many other parts of the memoir, Ancco's drawing in this violent scene is set in charcoal, lacks detail and preciseness, and is abstract and cartoony. Although Jinju's face is slightly exposed in one of the panels, it hardly suggests any expression (not even fear). Rather, Jinju appears almost non-human. It is as though readers are asked to observe the scene from a distance with only limited visual information. Images in the panels are viewed from a distance, and all readers get to see are the backs of characters (the father beating up Jinju and the mother and sister trying to stop him), while Jinju is almost completely invisible. That is, the ways in which images are shot and drawn in this scene strongly suggest, and even encourage, that readers stay outside the scene and take an observer position. This position, in fact, greatly enables readers' confrontation with the scene. Reading fiction in any literary form is made possible in part because it provides a safe place in which readers can confront disturbing feelings and experiences without being paralyzed by them. Readers' participation in the fictional world, in other words, "is a compromise between the first-person and the third-person perspective." Readers, in their literary experience, mentally simulate the minds of characters and their worlds and even transport themselves into these worlds, but they remain simultaneously conscious "of being external observers" in order not to "trespass the fragile boundary that separates pleasure from pain."[71]

Ancco's positioning of her characters, specific drawing style, and use of distant camera shots, as well as their overall impact on readerly positioning, together amount to maintaining this very "fragile boundary" for readers. As a result, readers can confront the disturbing violence without having to experience personal distress, while simultaneously being attached to and actively simulating the scene. This delicate balance between the first-person (active simulator) and third-person (distant observer) perspectives can be orchestrated effectively in comics because this medium facilitates readers' active cognitive engagement by gutters, the empty space between panels, and invites "closure," the work of observing the parts but perceiving the whole. The closure constantly occurring in gutters allows readers of comics to "connect [disconnected parts] and mentally construct a continuous, unified reality."[72] Thanks to this push (positioning of readers as observers) -pull (active mental processing and closure in gutters) mechanism of the memoir, Ancco's readers are able to keep a somewhat objective distance from Jinju while also fostering strong concern for her. The empathetic readability of Junju's "horror story," hence, increases.

Ancco's cartoony drawing style deserves further consideration in this very context. Scott McCloud calls cartoon drawing in comics an "iconic abstraction"[73] and explains that cartoon drawing abstracts an image, rids it of details and specificities, and increases the universality of the image. This is why comics artists often deploy cartoony faces, as these faces are easier for readers to identify with and project themselves upon. Ancco's cartoony faces, however, are simultaneously exaggerated and somewhat unsettling in such a way that they provoke disturbingly ambiguous feelings in readers' minds. Moreover, these faces are often situated against backgrounds and environments that tend to defamiliarize readers. For instance, in one particular panel, Jinju appears with her best friend, Jungae, and other classmates. They have gathered after school to smoke, drink, and play cards. The room, where the characters are cramped together, is characteristically dark and bleak. While all faces of the characters in the panel are abstract, cartoony, and lack specificity, seemingly inviting universalization and easier projection for readers, their empty gazes and the cigarettes in their hands and mouths also distinctively alienate these faces from readers. The school uniform that Jinju and her friends are wearing in the panel also makes a stark contrast with their demeanor and environment. The consequence, again, is the disquieting combination of the familiar (provoking first-person perspectives) and the strange (provoking third-person perspectives) that asks readers to approach the characters and their actions and circumstances with caution.

This ambivalent caution is much needed when evaluating the domestic violence that Jinju endures while growing up. Although domestic violence, teen prostitution, and juvenile delinquency are by no means exclusively Korean phenomena, Ancco's visual and verbal choices demand that readers evaluate Jinju's ruthlessly violent father with careful cultural considerations in the context of Korean family structure and dynamics. Almost after each scene of the father's violence, the present-day Jinju (as the autobiographical narrator) comments on the experience in retrospect in order to offer more context for and to defend her father's behavior: "Even if my father was harsh and beat me up, I never blamed him. ... Any parent would have done the same thing."[74] The author's explicit ethical assessment of the violence through the voice of her stand-in protagonist/narrator may be disturbing to many readers, but it is worth noting that the author contextualizes the ethics of violence more squarely within the family relation: "*Any parent* would have done the same thing" (my emphasis). Korean society, despite its rapid modernization and Westernization, is still largely governed by the Confucian values that recognize family as the key social unit. This is not surprising given the hardships that Koreans collectively went though during the "first part of the twentieth century, including colonial occupation and civil war, [which] left many Koreans in situations where the family was the only social unit that they could rely on."[75] This strong emphasis on the family has led to what Kyung-sup Chang calls "instrumental familism," a complete devotion to family "as an instrument for its members' social competition for status, wealth, and power."[76] Even in today's modern Korean society, instrumental familism is still common and dominant especially as the economy grows and competition among people becomes more and more severe; instrumental familism is centered on the right behaviors and strict disciplines that are believed to advance members of the family. It is within this uniquely Korean approach to family that Jinju's evaluation of her father's violence can be interpreted.

Of course, this ethical reading of the father and his action can still be disturbing to many readers who regard family more as an emotional and psychological buffer and a source of comfort.[77] Moreover, readers unfamiliar with the memoir's cultural context (i.e., non-Korean readers reading the memoir in translation) are more likely to find Jinju's ethical reading of the father and his violence disagreeable. This raises an interesting question about the rhetorical relationship between the author and readers, that is: To what extent can the author shape narrative experience of his/her readers and direct them to agree with his/her authorial message and intention? This question is more complicated when it comes to a text in translation where the author and readers have to cross not only the rhetorical boundary, but linguistic, cultural, and geographical borders in order to find each other in the same place. Indeed Peter Rabinowitz considers the author–reader relationship and notes that the author "cannot begin to fill up a blank page without making assumptions about the readers' beliefs, knowledge, and familiarity with conventions."[78] Rabinowitz thus concludes that authors "design their books rhetorically for some more or less specific hypothetical audiences" and calls this hypothetical audience the "authorial audience."[79] In other words, authors construct their authorial audience based on a wide range of assumptions including, for instance, widespread cultural conventions, and try to draw them into "a particular social/interpretive community" and invite them "to read in a particularly socially constituted way that is shared by the author and his or her expected readers."[80] Likewise, in order to engage the audience with her ethical reading of the father, Ancco has to persuade her readers, especially those from outside the Korean cultural context, to give up on their freedom as flesh and blood readers and to modify their cultural and ethical conventions—that is, to ultimately take up the position of Ancco's authorial audience.

For instance, after another scene of ruthless violence by her father, Jinju, as the narrator/writer of her memoir, steps into the narrative again. This time she is in her office working on what is supposed to be the very graphic memoir that readers are reading. As she draws, Jinju again defends her father: "There wasn't anything else my father could have done. Also, if Jungae had a father like mine, I probably would not have lost her."[81] The following chapter of the memoir focuses on Jungae as she, free from any parental scrutiny, leaves her home and school, starts working as a hostess at a bar, and eventually goes missing. Ancco's decision to present the authorial Jinju in her office and focus the narrative on the downfall of Jungae right after the scene of Jinju's father's abusive violence is deliberate and strategic. On the one hand, Jinju's authorial presence as the author of the memoir, who is simultaneously drawing it as readers read it, increases intimacy between Jinju and readers, thereby helping readers more easily identify with Jinju's perspective. It also proves that Jinju was right about defending her father, as the juxtaposition between herself and Jungae undoubtedly indicates. Authorial reading (reading from a position of the authorial audience) is inevitably tied to how successfully author guides readers' comprehension through his/her specific construction of the narrative. Such narrative construction offers cues to readers, and they infer authorial intention based on these cues and fill the gaps in order to make sense of the narrative and its intention. Ancco, through her careful crafting of images, page layout, and narrative progression, actively facilitates "extrapersonal" and "extracommunal"[82] reading by the authorial audience and guides her readers to step into her own social and interpretive community.

Ancco ends her memoir with less verbal specificity and direction. As an autobiographical narrator, Ancco reflects on her past, and she comments, "I no longer belong to the past. Fun memories are now the source of my stories, while I have already erased all bad memories."[83] Ancco concludes by explaining this was why she could not say anything when, on a bus one day, she accidentally ran into Jungae, with her baby on her back. Given that Jungae got on the bus in a red-light district, her life has gone for the worst. In a single elongated frame, readers see Jungae from behind. The baby is peacefully asleep and makes a stark contrast with the dark and bleak background of the panel that seems to devour up Jungae's fatigued and worn-out figure. At the right bottom of the panel, a caption notes: "It was horrifying that you were still living there."[84]

The narrative then shifts back to the past. Jinju and Jungae are together in a dark, cluttered room. Jungae is wearing make-up, and her dress indicates that she is working as a hostess at a bar. Jinju asks Jungae to come back soon, and Jungae responds, "I will make lots of money and come back."[85]

On the final two pages of the memoir right after this scene, temporal and spatial boundaries collide as strikingly similar images of a younger and an older Jinju, both captured from behind her, are placed right next to each other. In these two single-image panels, without gutters and verbal cues, Jinju's face is inaccessible, but her body posture (with her head tilted down and her back crouched) conveys the sense of guilt, shame, and regret—Jinju on the left side, for not having stopped Jungae when she was stepping into a world too dangerous and mature for her, and Jinju on the right side, for having ignored Jungae when she finally encountered her years later.

Ancco's decision to end her narrative visually rather than verbally is especially compelling due to the lyricality added to the graphic memoir. Although Ancco's memoir includes a story of change and seemingly significant improvement in Jinju's life, the narrative's overall progression can be said to be lyric. That is, the story of change and improvement in Jinju's circumstances is used in the service of Ancco's revelation of the more static psychological condition of Jinju's life. Although Jinju herself declares that she no longer belongs to her past, the final two images of the memoir strongly demonstrate that Jinju's interiority is governed by the unspoken continuity between her past and present. The consistent use of charcoal-soaked pages throughout the memoir also contributes to establishing dominant moods of stasis and bleakness against which Jinju's state of mind can be comprehended. What is especially important about this lyric quality of the memoir is that this attribute significantly influences readers' attitudes and positions with regard to Jinju. Jim Phelan explains that in lyric progressions, "[o]ur judgments and emotions focus not on character's choices and what they mean for what does and does not happen to them but rather on the progressive revelation of characters and their static situations."[86] Moreover, in some lyric progressions, "judgment drops out of our response to be replaced by sympathetic identification: rather than viewing the speaker from an observer position, we take on his or her perspective."[87] The juxtaposition of the two images at the end of the memoir, then, is not only indicative of Jinju's inner life, but also how readers may have to evaluate Jinju and her own sense of guilt implicitly implied by the absence of words. Readers such as Ancco's implied/authorial audience, being influenced by the lyric progression of the memoir, take on Jinju's perspective and reach a very sympathetic identification with her.

As Golnar Nabizadeh notes in "Vision and Precarity in Marjane Satrapi's *Persepolis*," most graphic narratives are "polyphonic in structure," as evident in the "co-constitutive relationship between the recitative-the authorial narrative and the diegetic text, usually in the form of speech bubbles." This polyphonic nature of graphic narratives contributes to creating a space for the past and present to exist mutually and simultaneously on the same page, and even panel, while the images accompanied by written words "generate multiple layers of meaning."[88] Interestingly, the final two pages of *Bad Friend* stay away from this very polyphonic structure that characterizes most graphic narratives and, instead, generates meaningful silence in the minds of readers. The single elongated frames on both pages, with neither gutters nor the blending of authorial narrative and diegetic text, suggest that rather than generating multiple meanings or judgments, readers see and feel Jinju's interiority from her own perspective. The silence that Jinju kept in the past and in the present resonates in the panel space and also beyond the panels, that is, in the minds of readers. Ancco introduces somber and quiet sense making in the memoir's last two pages, which ultimately fosters empathetic feelings for all "bad" characters with bad behaviors, the rebellious and reckless Jinju and Jungae, as well as Jinju's violent father.

Both Han Kang's *The Vegetarian* and Ancco's *Bad Friend* powerfully engage readers cognitively, emotionally, and ethically. They also demonstrate creativity, innovation, and the reach of Korean literary narratives in various forms that are indeed transcultural and transnational. In the meantime, the uniquely Korean context of both texts demands that the transnational/cultural reading of narratives is always accompanied by sensitivity for cultural and national specificities and attempts at stepping into the author's authorial audience. Such sensitivity and attempts will make for a possible extracultural and extrapersonal narrative experience that can be productively de-familiarizing and possibly renew our own limited pair of eyes.

Notes

1 Han Kang's novel was first published in Korean in 2007. Its English translation by Deborah Smith was published in 2015.
2 Ancco's graphic memoir was first published in Korean in 2012. Its English translation by Janet Hong was published in 2016.
3 Lina Jang, "Reading in South Korea Hits New Low," *Korean Biz Wire*, February 5, 2018, http://koreabizwire.com/reading-in-south-korea-hits-new-low/110153.
4 The novel was published in 2009 in South Korea and translated in English by Chi-young Kim, winning the 2011 Man Asian Literary Prize; the book's popular reception is clear as it was chosen by Oprah Winfrey to be one of her "18 Books to Watch for in April 2011" and by Amazon as one of its "Best Books of the Month: April 2011."
5 This children's book was first published in 2000 and was translated by Chi-Young Kim in 2013.
6 Dennis Abrams,"Examining Korean Literature in Translation and International Reach," *Publishing Perspectives*, January 18, 2017, https://publishingperspectives.com/2017/01/korean-translation-literature-globalization/.
7 Dennis Abrams, "Korean Literature Needs More Skilled Translators," *Publishing Perspectives*, July 7, 2014, https://publishingperspectives.com/2014/07/korean-literature-needs-more-skilled-translators/.
8 Im Eun-byel, "Like BTS, Can Korean Literature Be Globally Embraced?," *The Korean Herald*, September 6, 2018, www.koreaherald.com/view.php?ud=20180906000577.
9 I use the term in the sense of Russian formalism to mean the process of defamiliarization. For more, see Viktor Shklovsky, *Theory of Prose* (Chicago: Dalkey Archive Press, 1993).
10 Suzanne Keen, "A Theory of Narrative Empathy," *Narrative* 14, no. 3 (2006): 208.
11 Focalization is the perspective or point of view "in terms of which the narrated situations and events are presented; the perceptual or conceptual position in terms of which they are rendered." See Gerald Prince, *Dictionary of Narratology* (Lincoln: University of Nebraska Press, 1989), 31.
12 한강[Han Kang], 채식주의자[*The Vegetarian*] (Seoul: Chang-bi, 2007), 10.
13 Han Kang, *The Vegetarian* (New York: Hogarth, 2015), 11.
14 The Man Booker International Prize is awarded to both the writer and translator of the novel.
15 Claire Armitstead, "Lost in (mis)translation? English take on Korean novel has critics up in arms," *The Guardian*, January 15, 2018, www.theguardian.com/books/booksblog/2018/jan/15/lost-in-mistranslation-english-take-on-korean-novel-has-critics-up-in-arms.
16 Ibid.
17 Ibid.

18 See Susan Bassnett, *Translation, History and Culture* (New York: Continuum, 1998).
19 Edwin Genztler, "Translation, Poststructuralism, and Power," in *Translation and Power*, ed. Edwin Gentzler and Maria Tymoczko (Amherst: University of Massachusetts Press, 2002), 216.
20 Charles Montgomery, "Korea: A Country of One's Own? Thoughts on Han Kang's Booker Victory," *Korean Literature in translation*, May 18, 2016, www.ktlit.com/korea-a-country-of-ones-own-thoughts-on-han-kangs-booker-victory/.
21 For more on the discussion on translation and its many political implications, See "Translation Matters" in Frederick Luis Aldama, *Why the Humanities Matter* (Austin: University of Texas Press, 2008).
22 Rincy Chandran and Geetha Pai, "The Flowering of Human Consciousness: An Ecofeminist Reading of Han Kang's *The Vegetarian* and *The Fruit of My Woman*," *International Journal of English and Literature* 7, no. 4 (2017), 22.
23 Paola Bica, "*The Vegetarian* by Han Kang: A Postmodern Allegory for Women's Fight for Power and Freedom," accessed March 3, 2020, www.academia.edu/38451676/The_Vegetarian_by_Han_Kang_A_postmodern_allegory_for_women_s_fight_for_power_and_freedom.
24 The authorial audience is the hypothetical audience for whom the author composes his/her text. See "Introduction" for a more detailed explanation on how I conceptualize the authorial audience position according to the rhetorical approach to narrative.
25 Jongyon Hwang, "A Postnational Turn in Contemporary Korean Literature," *World Literature Today* 85, no. 1 (2010), 51.
26 Kang, 31.
27 Ibid., 33.
28 Porter Abbott, "Unreadable Minds and the Captive Reader," *Style* 42, no. 4 (2008), 451.
29 Brian McHale, *Postmodernist Fiction* (New York: Routledge, 1987), 211.
30 David Herman defines storyworlds as "mental models of who did what to and with whom, when, where, why, and in what fashion in the world to which recipients relocate." See David Herman, *Story Logic* (Lincoln: Nebraska, 2002), 9.
31 Kang, 20. Yeong-hye's interior monologues are italicized in the novel.
32 External focalization is "a type of focalization or point of view whereby the information conveyed is mostly limited to what the characters do and say and there is never any direct indication of what they think or feel." See Gerald Prince, *Dictionary of Narratology* (Lincoln: University of Nebraska Press, 1989), 29.
33 Internal focalization is "a type of focalization whereby information is conveyed in terms of a character's (conceptual or perceptual) point of view or perspective." See Gerald Prince, *Dictionary of Narratology* (Lincoln: University of Nebraska Press, 1989), 45.

34 Kang, 56.
35 My use of the term "private text" derives from Susan Lanser's "Toward a Feminist Narratology," *Style* 20, no. 3 (Fall 1986): 341–363.
36 The narratee is the person inside the text to whom the narrator is speaking, although the narratee does not have to be fully characterized or identified.
37 Jim Phelan, *Somebody Telling Somebody Else* (Columbus: Ohio State University Press, 2017), 8.
38 Kang, 45.
39 Ibid., 47.
40 Mee-hee Kong, "Rethinking Women's Status and Liberation in Korea," *United Nations Public Administration Network*, accessed February 5, 2020, www.semanticscholar.org/paper/Rethinking-women's-status-and-liberation-in-Korea-Kong/d90d64a69c91fa8259652732b360e97e3281ba23.
41 Kim Arin, "Communal Dipping, 'A Wartime Eating Habit with Health Consequences,'" *The Korea Herald*, July 18, 2019, www.koreaherald.com/view.php?ud=20190718000452&ACE_SEARCH=1.
42 Wolfgang Iser, *The Implied Reader* (Baltimore: Johns Hopkins University Press, 1974), xii.
43 Brian Richardson, "Singular Text, Multiple Implied Readers," *Style* 41, no. 3 (2007), 259.
44 Ibid., 262.
45 Interestingly, many of my white American students unfamiliar with Korean culture and family dynamics described the scene as "overly dramatic," "contrived," "too emotional," and "thematically oriented."
46 Ibid., 263.
47 Kang, 31.
48 Brian Richardson, *Unnatural Narrative: Theory, History, and Practice* (Columbus: Ohio State University Press, 2015).
49 Jan Alber "Impossible Storyworlds—and What to Do with Them," *Storyworlds: A Journal of Narrative Studies* 1 (2009): 79–96.
50 Kang, 48.
51 Part 2 of the novel is narrated by a third-person narrator, while Yeong-hye's brother-in-law operates as the focalizer of the narrative. His focalization reveals how he objectifies and sexualizes Yeong-hye.
52 Kang, 95.
53 Bica, 5.
54 Kang, 133.
55 Bica, 5.
56 Kang, 41.
57 Ibid., 187.
58 Ibid., 188.
59 Keen, 208.
60 Marianne Hirsch, *The Generation of Postmemory: Writing and Visual Culture After the Holocaust* (New York: Columbia University Press, 2012).

61 Judith Butler, "Photography, War, Outrage," *PMLA* 120, no. 3 (May 2005): 822–827.
62 Hillary Chute, "The Shadow of a Past Time: History and Graphic Representation in *Maus*," *Twentieth-Century Literature* 52, no. 2 (Summer 2006): 199–230.
63 Gillian Whitlock, "Autographics: The Seeing "I" of the Comics," *Modern Fiction Studies* 52, no. 4 (Winter 2006), 965.
64 Jared Gardner, *Projections: Comics and the History of Twenty-First Century Storytelling* (Palo Alto: Stanford University Press, 2012), 6.
65 Keen, 208.
66 Golnar Nabizadeh, "Vision and Precarity in Marjane Satrapi's Persepolis," *Women's Studies Quarterly* 44, no. 1–2 (2016), 153.
67 For more, Mieke Bal, *Narratology: Introduction to the Theory of Narrative* (Toronto: University of Toronto Press, 1997) and Shlomith Rimmon-Kenan, *Narrative Fiction: Contemporary Poetics* (New York: Routledge, 2002).
68 "Talking, Thinking, and Seeing in Pictures: Narration, Focalization, and Ocularization in Comics Narratives," accessed April 23, 2010, https://madinkbeard.com/archives/talking-thinking-and-seeing-in-pictures-narration-focalization-and-ocularization-in-comics-narratives.
69 Ibid.
70 Ancco, 11.
71 Marie-Laure Ryan, "Will New Media Produce New Narratives?" *Narrative across Media: The Languages of Storytelling*, ed. Marie-Laure Ryan (Lincoln: University of Nebraska Press, 2004), 347.
72 Scott McCloud, *Understanding Comics: The Invisible Art* (New York: William Morrow Paperbacks, 1994), 67.
73 Ibid., 54.
74 Ancco, 31.
75 McCloud, 67.
76 John Finch and Seung-kyung Kim, "The Korean Family in Transition," in *Routledge Handbook of Korean Culture and Society*, ed. Youna Kim (New York: Routledge, 2016), 138.
77 The unit of family with more emphasis on affect and comfort can be called "affectionate familism." For more, see Chang Kyung-Sup, "Compressed Modernity and Korean Families: Accidental Pluralism in Family Ideology" in *Korean Families: Continuity and Change*, ed. Chang Kyung-Sup (Seoul: Seoul National University Press, 2011).
78 Peter Rabinowitz, *Before Reading: Narrative Conventions and the Politics of Interpretation* (Columbus: Ohio State University, 1998), 21.
79 Ibid.
80 Ibid., 22.
81 Ancco, 77–78.
82 Rabinowitz, 26.
83 Ancco, 158–159.

84 Ibid.
85 Ibid., 173.
86 Jim Phelan, *Living to Tell About It* (Ithaca: Cornell University Press, 2005), 10.
87 Ibid.
88 Nabizadeh, 5.

Bibliography

Abrams, Dennis. "Examining Korean Literature in Translation and International Reach." *Publishing Perspectives*. January 18, 2017. https://publishingperspectives.com/2017/01/korean-translation-literature-globalization/.

———. "Korean Literature Needs More Skilled Translators." *Publishing Perspectives*. July 7, 2014. https://publishingperspectives.com/2014/07/korean-literature-needs-more-skilled-translators/.

Abbott, Porter. "Unreadable Minds and the Captive Reader." *Style* 42, no. 4 (2008): 448–466.

Alber, Jan. "Impossible Storyworlds—and What to Do with Them." *Storyworlds: A Journal of Narrative Studies* 1 (2009): 79–96.

Aldama, Frederick Luis. *Why the Humanities Matter*. Austin: University of Texas Press, 2008.

Armitstead, Claire. "Lost in (Mis)translation? English take on Korean Novel has Critics Up in Arms." *The Guardian*. January 15, 2018. www.theguardian.com/books/booksblog/2018/jan/15/lost-in-mistranslation-english-take-on-korean-novel-has-critics-up-in-arms.

Arin, Kim. "Communal Dipping, 'A Wartime Eating Habit with Health Consequences.'" *The Korea Herald*. July 18, 2019. www.koreaherald.com/view.php?ud=20190718000452&ACE_SEARCH=1.

Bassnett, Susan. *Translation, History and Culture*. New York: Continuum, 1998.

Bica, Paola. "*The Vegetarian* by Han Kang: A Postmodern Allegory for Women's Fight for Power and Freedom." Accessed March 3, 2020. www.academia.edu/38451676/The_Vegetarian_by_Han_Kang_A_postmodern_allegory_for_women_s_fight_for_power_and_freedom.

Butler, Judith. "Photography, War, Outrage." *PMLA* 120, no. 3 (2005): 822–827.

Chandran, Rincy and Geetha Pai. "The Flowering of Human Consciousness: An Ecofeminist Reading of Han Kang's *The Vegetarian* and *The Fruit of My Woman*." *International Journal of English and Literature* 7, no. 4 (2017): 21–28.

Chute, Hillary. "The Shadow of a Past Time: History and Graphic Representation in *Maus*." *Twentieth-Century Literature* 52, no. 2 (2006): 199–230.

Eun-byel, Im. "Like BTS, Can Korean Literature Be Globally Embraced?" *The Korean Herald*. September 6, 2018. www.koreaherald.com/view.php?ud=20180906000577.

Finch, John and Seung-kyung Kim. "The Korean Family in Transition." In *Routledge Handbook of Korean Culture and Society*, edited by Youna Kim, 134–148. New York: Routledge, 2016.
Gardner, Jared. *Projections: Comics and the History of Twenty-First Century Storytelling*. Palo Alto: Stanford University Press, 2012.
Genztler, Edwin. "Translation, Poststructuralism, and Power." In *Translation and Power*, edited by Edwin Gentzler and Maria Tymoczko, 185–195. Amherst: University of Massachusetts Press, 2002.
Hwang, Jongyon. "A Postnational Turn in Contemporary Korean Literature." *World Literature Today* 85, no. 1 (2010): 50–52.
Hirsch, Marianne. *The Generation of Postmemory: Writing and Visual Culture After the Holocaust*. New York: Columbia University Press, 2012.
Iser, Wolfgan. *The Implied Reader*. Baltimore: Johns Hopkins University Press, 1974.
Jang, Lina. "Reading in South Korea Hits New Low." *Korean Biz Wire*. February 5, 2018. http://koreabizwire.com/reading-in-south-korea-hits-new-low/110153.
Keen, Suzanne. "A Theory of Narrative Empathy." *Narrative* 14, no. 3 (2006): 207–236.
Kong, Mee-hee. "Rethinking Women's Status and Liberation in Korea." *United Nations Public Administration Network*. Accessed February 5, 2020. www.semanticscholar.org/paper/Rethinking-women's-status-and-liberation-in-Korea-Kong/d90d64a69c91fa8259652732b360e97e3281ba23.
Kang, Han. *The Vegetarian*. New York: Hogarth, 2015.
한강[Han Kang]. 채식주의자 [*The Vegetarian*]. Seoul: Chang-bi, 2007.
Lanser, Susan. "Toward a Feminist Narratology." *Style* 20, no. 3 (1986): 341–363.
McCloud, Scott. *Understanding Comics: The Invisible Art*. New York: William Morrow Paperbacks, 1994.
McHale, Brian. *Postmodernist Fiction*. New York: Routledge, 1987.
Montgomery, Charles. "Korea: A Country of One's Own? Thoughts on Han Kang's Booker Victory." *Korean Literature in Translation*. May 18, 2016. www.ktlit.com/korea-a-country-of-ones-own-thoughts-on-han-kangs-booker-victory/.
Nabizadeh, Golnar. "Vision and Precarity in Marjane Satrapi's Persepolis." *Women's Studies Quarterly* 44, no. 1-2 (2016): 152–167.
Phelan, Jim. *Somebody Telling Somebody Else*. Columbus: Ohio State University Press, 2017.
———. *Living to Tell About It*. Ithaca: Cornell University Press, 2005.
Rabinowitz, Peter. *Before Reading: Narrative Conventions and the Politics of Interpretation*. Columbus: Ohio State University, 1998.
Richardson, Brian. "Singular Text, Multiple Implied Readers." *Style* 41, no. 3 (2007): 259–274.
Richardson, Brian. *Unnatural Narrative: Theory, History, and Practice*. Columbus: Ohio State University Press, 2015.

Ryan, Marie-Laure. "Will New Media Produce New Narratives?" In *Narrative Across Media: The Languages of Storytelling*, edited by Marie-Laure Ryan, 337–359. Lincoln: University of Nebraska Press, 2004.

"Talking, Thinking, and Seeing in Pictures: Narration, Focalization, and Ocularization in Comics Narratives." Accessed April 23, 2010. https://madinkbeard.com/archives/talking-thinking-and-seeing-in-pictures-narration-focalization-and-ocularization-in-comics-narratives.

Whitlock, Gillian. "Autographics: The Seeing 'I' of the Comics." *Modern Fiction Studies* 52, no. 4 (2006): 965–979.

2 Korean webtoon wave

Narratological, technological, and medial innovations of Korean digital comics

Manga, comics created in Japan using the Japanese language and style that developed in the late nineteenth century, has long been a representative cultural product of Japan.[1] Manga's popularity and success in the European and US markets since the 1970s have led many to mistakenly use the term as a synonym for Asian comics. This misunderstanding has resulted in overlooking the variety and diversity of other comics originated from different parts of Asia, including, for instance, *manhwa*, comics of Korea that became popular in the nation during the 1920s.[2] The dominance of manga in the global market, however, is diminishing with the increasing popularity of Korean webtoon, the Korean term for comics created for the purpose of being published and read online, both domestically and globally. For instance, Naver, Korea's major search engine offering the largest webtoon services in the country, reached 18 million global readers in 2014, 2 years after it launched its global webtoon service, Line Webtoon.[3] This fast growth of webtoon in the global market compellingly supports the seemingly bold statement by Didier Borg, the chief executive officer of French online comics website Delitoon, at the world's first webtoon forum in 2014: "webtoon will replace manga."[4]

This chapter examines webtoon as another significant media and cultural product from South Korea that is a major part of the Korean Wave and deserves further analytical and theoretical attention. In my attempt to shed light on the diverse (themes, characters, styles) and innovative (technological, narratological, medium-specific) nature of Korean webtoons, I offer a close reading of two individual webtoons, the *Dr. P Series* and *Encountered*, and focus on the systematic ways in which these webtoons engage readers and inform their reading experience with their unique technological and narratological properties and medium specificities. Scholarly attention to webtoon has steadily increased for the past five to ten years. The scope of existing scholarship, however, is limited primarily to explaining the cultural and social background of South Korea that has accelerated the development and popularity of webtoon: using statistics,[5] putting webtoon and its impact in a broad conversation with media and cultural studies,[6] and situating the development of webtoon within the genealogy of Korean literature more generally.[7] While these existing studies offer comprehensive and highly informative overviews of the webtoon industry at large, their big-picture approach inevitably misses individual efforts that make possible this industry in the first place, namely, the creativity and innovations of webtoon creators and the myriad ways—using artistic, technological, and narratological tools at their disposal—in which they guide readers' engagement with their work.

Although I offer some general background information about the birth and growth of webtoon and its globalization, my approach to webtoon in this chapter is different, as it closely analyzes the selected webtoons with a distinct analytical and theoretical emphasis for each. For the *Dr. P Series*, I challenge the popular idea in literary studies that readable fictional minds are crucial to the comprehension of fiction.[8] I posit that the author of *Dr. P Series* consciously erases readable minds by making deliberate artistic and narratological choices, and this absence of readable minds is at the center of the new mode of reading that the *Dr. P Series* facilitates through its digital mediality. In my discussion of *Encountered*, on the other hand, I pay greater attention to the techno-mediated narrative environment of the webtoon and its numerous technological innovations. These include, among other things, the use of augmented reality and 360-degree panorama and facial recognition. Ultimately, I show how the webtoon allows readers the feeling of stepping into the webtoon's simulated world and makes possible for them the highly embodied reading experience. The Korean webtoon industry is diverse, dynamic, and rapidly changing. My reading of the two webtoons in this chapter avoids generalizing what Korean webtoon is and how it works. It also intends to draw attention back to the core of its industry, the producer/creator and reader/consumer—that is, how webtoon creators specifically construct their visual-techno narratives in order to engage readers, and how readers consume and ultimately inform and complete these webtoons through their active reading and simulation.

Webtoon 101: the art of transmedia storytelling

The term "trans" as a prefix denotes across, beyond, and through. Transmedia, when used by itself, then, can simply mean across media.

Transmedia storytelling, conversely, represents "a process where integral elements of a fiction get dispersed systematically across multiple delivery channels for the purpose of creating a unified and coordinated entertainment experience."[9] The 2005 filmic adaptation of Jane Austin's 1813 novel *Pride and Prejudice*, for instance, showcases a practice of transmedia storytelling whereby readers–viewers are invited to explore different and yet continual representations of the same plot, characters, actions, and setting through "multiple delivery channels," novel (print) on the one hand and film (audiovisual) on the other hand. Transmedia storytelling has been a popular mode of storytelling in many areas of modern and popular cultural practices including, for instance, the film industry. According to a research commissioned by the Publishers Associations, "[f]ilm adaptations of books gross 44% more at the U.K. box office and a full 53% more worldwide than films from original screenplays." The same study also found that "43% of the top 20 highest grossing films in the UK from 2007 to 2016 were book-based and another 9% were based on comics."[10]

The growing prominence and popularity of transmedia storytelling are indicative of the highly adaptive and flexible nature of narrative and its intricate relationship to medium. What kind of meaning narrative produces and how it engages narrative recipients depend on what specific form and shape, that is, medium, narrative takes. After all, Marshall McLuhan was right when he famously said, "the medium is the message."[11] Questions concerning the relationship between narrative and medium become complicated, not only when elements of a narrative are dispersed across multiple delivery channels, but also when they are formed and reshaped by the convergence of media of different and often opposite natures. Media convergence, characterizing today's media innovation and experimentation, can be defined through "the layering, diversification, and interactivity of media" and contrasts with the digital revolution model "which assumed old media would be replaced by new media."[12] This reciprocal and mutual dependency of old and new media is at the center of media convergence and echoes Jay Bolter and Richard Grusin's concept of "remediation," wherein every medium "is developed as an attempt to remediate the deficiencies of another medium. ... Media need each other to function as media at all."[13] Webtoon's mode of storytelling captures transmedia storytelling in the context of media convergence—the convergence of digital media and comics, while the integral elements of narrative are dispersed systematically across the both delivery channels. As my analyses of the *Dr. P Series* and *Encountered* in the rest of this chapter will show, the intrinsic properties of digital and comics media contribute to the storytelling practices of the chosen webtoons. At the same time, these properties of media shape and are shaped by one another reciprocally and mutually in order to offer a new set of narrative and entertainment experience to readers, one that renews their mode of reading and perception.

According to Dal Yong Jin, the beginning of webtoon in Korea can be traced back to the late 1990s, when personal webpages were first launched in the country. Several cartoonists started to show their work on their webpages in order to escape "the pressure of having to fill up a page by uploading loosely configured drawings with ample margins that simply required scrolling" and to save on the expenses of production and marketing.[14] The term webtoon, however, officially appeared in the early 2000s with Korea's economic growth and expansion, particularly in the electronic sectors, and the resulting development of online connectivity in the country. In 2003, one of the major search engines in Korea Daum started to publish serially works by cartoonists Yoon Tae-ho and Kang Full, who were already attracting millions of viewers. Kang Full's webtoon *Apartment* also became the first online comics to be released as a movie. The rival search engine, Naver, launched its own webtoon service called Naver Webtoon in 2005 and by 2014, it was recorded that 6.2 million people visited Naver Webtoon to read various webtoons.[15] The webtoon industry, however, grew exponentially with the spread of smartphones in Korea. By 2012, the penetration rate of smartphones had already surpassed 67.6 percent. In 2018, 95 percent of the South Korean population was using a smartphone, "marking the highest level of smartphone ownership in the world."[16] Korea's webtoon industry is a clear beneficiary of these high Internet and smartphone penetration rates. Indeed by 2016, the country had "more than 4,000 digital comics series offered by more than 30 mobile webtoon platforms."[17] Virtually anyone can access a wide range of webtoons at any time and place, quickly searching for their favorite webtoon episodes and simply scrolling down touch screens of their handheld devices. In this environment of ubiquitous connectivity and an ever-growing need for new modes of storytelling, webtoons have become "one of Korea's fastest-growing writing platforms today."[18]

Several other factors have contributed to the growth and popularity of webtoons in Korea. First, the advanced technological environment of the country is coupled with the nation's social and cultural environment in such a way that Koreans turn to webtoons as a way to break from the severe competition and pressure of modern life. According to 2016 data compiled by the Organization for Economic Co-operation and Development (OECD), "South Korea has currently longer working hours than any other developed country: an average 2,069 hours per year, per worker." This has led the South Korean government to pass a law to reduce the nation's maximum working week from 68 hours to 52 hours, hoping "to boost the country's productivity and the number of children being born."[19] With hardly any time left for leisurely activity after long hours of work each day, many young Koreans seem to find great comfort in webtoons; each episode of any given webtoon takes only a few seconds to read, and Koreans, living in the most wired nation in the world, can access webtoons in any place, including on subways, as long as they have a few seconds and minutes to spare. Most Koreans in populated urban centers use public transportation to commute, and the long hours spent in this way prompt them to take out their smartphones and click on their favorite webtoon episodes, and new ones are uploaded weekly.

Second, webtoons' online platform helps maintain and encourage diversity and creativity of webtoons uploaded digitally. Compared to traditional print media, digital publishing is less exposed to rigorous and intrusive censorship, and webtoon writers therefore have more flexibility and freedom with their work. The popularity of "bad taste" webtoons and their use of violent and sensitive images and subject matters, which I elaborate on later in the chapter, is an example. Indeed, Naver offers 13 webtoon genres for readers to choose from, and these webtoons are vastly different from one another in terms of style (visual and verbal), themes, target age/gender, and so forth. Naver also capitalizes on the platform's technological system to ensure the diversity of the webtoons that they offer. Cha Jung-yoon, Naver's public relations officer, said in an interview how Naver's digital platform enables them to systematically enforce diversity and creativity of the works that they publish:

> We keep a 'line-up matrix' of current webtoons to find out which genres in which group and in which gender are underserved and accordingly select webtoons that can fill that void.[20]

Third, webtoons are simultaneously participatory and interactive. While both audience participation and interactivity characterize digital media and popular culture, as Henry Jenkins makes clear, there exists a distinct difference between them. Whereas interactivity is pre-programmed in such a way that user interaction leads to actual, measurable changes to media content being consumed (computer games, for instance), participation is high on fan culture, "where fans take the resources offered by a text and push it in a range of directions which are neither programmed nor authorized by the producers."[21] Interestingly, the comment section that appears underneath each webtoon episode facilitates participation and interactivity concurrently or, to put it differently, each episode of any given webtoon is programed in such a way that reader participation ultimately leads to reader interactivity, adding measurable changes to the subsequent episodes that follow. First, readers participate by simply writing their thoughts and suggestions in the comment section and rating their favorite webtoons and webtoon writers. They also participate, of course, by choosing to read a certain webtoon over the other. These participatory activities of webtoon readers, however, are highly measurable as they become immediate feedback for portal platforms to refer to in order to decide which webtoons will be selected to run for the next season. In other words, it is crucial for webtoon writers to be receptive to readers' participation and take their feedback into consideration when determining the course of the visual and verbal characteristics of their webtoons. As readers' participation leads to increasingly measurable and impactful interactivity, Korean webtoon has become an ever changing, dynamic, and cooperative reading and publishing industry with a high level of vitality that keeps both writers and readers of webtoon active, and creative.

Lastly, webtoon's digital medium constructs a narrative environment that is highly techno-mediated and engages readers in productively new ways. Narrative potentials of digital media are many. While narrative can be defined as "a mental representation of causally connected states and events that captures a segment in the history of a world and of its members," the logico-semantic characterization of narrative is "sufficiently abstract to be regarded as a cognitive universal but flexible enough to tolerate a wide range of variations."[22] Webtoon's distinct digital properties—multiple sensory and semiotic channels, interactive and reactive nature, and so forth—expand the very flexibility of narrative and its possible modes of mental representation, as well as the meaning and experience that it offers to readers. This is because, as Marie-Laure Ryan notes, "different media filter different aspects of narrative meaning. ... [T]he shape imposed on the message by the configuration of the pipeline affects in a crucial way the construction of the receiver's mental image."[23] The configuration of webtoon's digital "pipeline" is never static and ever-evolving and stimulates readers' minds and bodies in unusual and yet highly engaging ways—a point that I highlight in my analyses of the two webtoons.

The popularity of webtoon within Korea has led to its globalization. Daum launched its global service in 2014 by partnering with the US-based Tapas Media, offering English translations for some of their popular webtoons.[24] Meanwhile, its competitor, Naver, offers about twelve hundred English webtoons and five hundred Chinese webtoons through their global service Line Webtoon. The Korean government has also joined the effort to grow the nation's webtoon industry beyond its borders and initiated an online project, K-Webtoon, which "aims to construct [the] database of Korean webtoon and at the same time to play the role of a gate in introducing webtoon to the world."[25] The initiative through its website offers numerous webtoons in English free of charge and holds an international webtoon forum every year to introduce new works and artists to the world. Moreover, Korean webtoons can potentially contribute to the further growth of the Korean Wave more generally. While Korean dramas, movies, and popular music have been the major force for the spread of Korean popular culture, webtoon as a new cultural and media product can add fresh new energies to the Korean Wave. According to research conducted in 2014 with a focus group involving 16 Indonesians, participants between the ages of 20 and 40 answered that Korean dramas and movies generally lack creativity and diversity, as they have long been focusing on a limited range of themes and plots, and their modes of storytelling are more conventional. By contrast, Korean webtoons are diverse and innovative in themes, styles, and modes of storytelling. When this diversity is coupled with their online-based accessibility and spreadability, Korean webtoons can help fill the very void that the current Korean Wave is facing by offering new media content that can be adapted by more traditional media platforms. For instance, between 2006 and 2013, 11 popular webtoons were made into successful films.[26]

Dr. P Series: consumption of unreadable minds and ugly feelings

Literary scholars such as Lisa Zunshine, Alan Palmer, and George Butte have been engaging with cognitive and neuro sciences as well as cognitive and social psychology in order to illuminate what happens when we read, and why we read at all. Drawing on the idea that "we have an evolved craving to read the minds of others and a corollary craving for the kind of narrative action that catalyzes this reading of minds,"[27] these theorists consider reading fiction as an act of reading and misreading minds of characters in the fictional world. In *Why We Read Fiction,* for instance, Lisa Zunshine discusses the folk-psychology term "Theory of Mind" (ToM) and defines it as an innate human capacity that seeks to understand "people's behavior in terms of their thoughts, feelings, beliefs, and desires."[28] The triggering of ToM is an important aspect of how and why we read fiction. When we read fiction, we naturally associate characters with a range of possible thoughts, feelings, and desires and refer to them as "cues" to interpret characters' minds and further predict their actions:

> We make sense of what we read by investing the flimsy verbal constructions that we generously call *characters* with a potential for a variety of thoughts, feelings, and desires and then looking for the 'cues' that would allow us to guess at their feelings and thus predict their actions.[29]

Although assumptions we make about others' minds can often be incorrect, Zunshine points out that reading minds and making attributions about them is the default way by which we construct and navigate our social environment, a practice that we apply when we navigate a fictional environment.

ToM (or mind reading) follows a procedure that is highly logical, specific, and deliberate. Indeed, when readers first encounter fictional characters, they locate potential responses to them within a scope that contains "an infinitely rich array of interpretations." In the course of narrative, however, readers narrow down these interpretations by "organiz[ing] information in specific ways" based on the cues provided by the author.[30] This cognitive act of mind reading is especially important in fiction because it ultimately offers a basis for empathy, a vicarious, spontaneous sharing of affect that can allow for a more immersive, engaging, and altruistic reading experience for readers. According to Suzanne Keen in "A Theory of Narrative Empathy," empathy can be stimulated "by witnessing another's emotional state, by hearing about another's condition, or even by reading."[31] Because empathy occurs when we can mirror and further identify with what we believe to be the emotion of others in a particular condition or context, that is, through the act of mind reading, empathy and mind reading are closely interrelated and, as Zunshine says, make literature possible and perhaps more meaningful.

Questions, then, arise when readers face fictional characters whose minds are hard to access and thus rendered incomprehensible. What do readers do if there are not enough coherent narrative details in the text, and the "cues" that supposedly guide readers' sense-making and mind reading, are nowhere to be found? Given the close relationship between mind reading and empathy, readers' inability to read the minds of characters will also have noticeable consequences on their affective responses to fiction. This is precisely what happens in the *Dr. P Series* by Korean webtoon writer Gyui Gyui (hereafter GG). In the case of the *Dr. P Series*, these questions become more complicated because the narrative of the webtoon, while presenting characters whose actions and minds are hard to make sense of and identify with, focuses on eliciting emotions that are so aversive and negative. These emotions, rather than inviting empathy, are more likely to distress readers and may even lead them to stop reading all together. The popularity of the *Dr. P Series*, however, indicates that there is something else at work in this webtoon that makes it highly engaging and entertaining. Therefore, in my first case study, I re-visit the cognitivist idea that readable minds and empathy arouse narrative desire and enable readers' capacity to engage with fiction. To do so, I investigate how the visual and medium specificities of the *Dr. P Series* create a narrative environment wherein the absence of readable minds and empathy engages readers.

The visual and verbal characteristics of the *Dr. P Series*, which I detail in my analysis of the webtoon, qualify genre conventions of bad-taste webtoons. The term "bad taste" was first used online by netizens (online citizens) and can be loosely translated into anything that is unconventional, absurd, ridiculous, nonsensical, or ironic. Before the term became common among younger users of the Internet, a comparable term, *mak-jang*, meaning a dead-end and nonsensical plot, was more frequently employed to describe televisual dramas that included characters, events, actions, and causalities used to dramatize the story to an extreme—falling in love with half-siblings unknowingly, killing daughter-in-law to help the success of the son, and so forth. Similarly, the bad-taste webtoon is a type of a comedy webtoon that is absurd, exaggerated, nonsensical, and free from formal and thematic conventions and restrictions. These webtoons are also drawn in cartoony, unprofessional, sketchy, non-realistic, and unsophisticated ways. Because bad-taste webtoons often use the visual and verbal that can be offensive, violent, and insensitive, many bad-taste webtoon artists employ User Create Contents (UCC) friendly community websites such as dcinside,[32] rather than major web portals, in order to upload and share their work, without having to worry about a censorship control. For instance, GG, one of the most famous bad-taste webtoon writers in Korea, has been both controversial and popular due to his overly explicit use of violence in his work. In 2012, after *Josun-ilbo*, a major newspaper company in Korea, criticized GG's series (set at a high school) for encouraging violence and bullying, Yahoo Korea, publisher of the series, issued a public apology and terminated publication.[33] GG then turned to his own personal website to continue his work, and his fans have been actively uploading and disseminating GG's bad-taste webtoons through numerous community websites. The popularity of

GG's work has also led to successful merchandizing of clothes, cups, and other items with his webtoon characters imprinted on them.

The *Dr. P Series* revolves around a superhero-looking character named "Dr. P," a mysterious physician who treats his patients with methods that are highly absurd and problematic, to say the least. The first episode starts with a patient walking into Dr. P's office complaining about a toothache. While both Dr. P and the unnamed patient are drawn in sketchy and unsophisticated lines, the patient looks a lot less significant than the doctor—being short, his face covered with wrinkles, and a toothbrush stuck in his bald head. As the patient asks for help, Dr. P suddenly breaks the patient's leg and tells him that he will be able to forget about the toothache due to the severe pain in his leg. Not surprisingly, the patient is horrified and struggles with even greater pain. In response to the patient's suffering, Dr. P now attacks the patient's spine and says, "Since I have broken your spine and destroyed your nerve system, you will no longer feel any pain in your leg." With a close-up shot of the patient's bloody and distorted face as a short preview for the next episode, the first episode of the series ends.[34]

Most readers are likely to find the visual and verbal of this particular episode cruel and unpleasant, but there is something about this episode that amuses readers and keeps them reading the episode. Even I cannot help laughing while reading the episode, without knowing fully why I am laughing and what I am laughing at. In fact, as I laugh, I feel guilty that I am amused by someone else's pain no matter that is fictional. Indeed, many cultural critics have pointed out that it is the "guilty pleasure" that draws readers to bad-taste webtoons.[35] Although most readers are aware of what is right and wrong and try to do what is right at all times, when the wrong is exaggerated, clumsily put together, and normalized, readers are likely to feel freer to do what they know they are not supposed to do in their real life—to be entertained by what is being marginalized (rightly so) as wrong and unethical. Readers' comments in the comment section of the episode reveal the ambivalent nature of their narrative experience: "I know this is so horrible, but it is also so fun." "Ridiculous, but truly genius." "This is so cool." And so forth. There are clearly an innocent victim and a violent aggressor in the episode, but it is difficult to understand or relate to any character's thought, behavior, or action. Dr. P's action and behavior are so incoherent, absurd, and out of context that readers will have a hard time attributing to him any motivation. The experience of the patient is equally challenging to make sense of and, hence, to empathize with. Even if readers notice his pain and may feel bad for him, this sympathetic feeling does not develop to empathy, the sharing of affect. Empathetic recognition requires that one notices and reads the feelings of others (which readers do in this episode), but empathy is also a situational, contextual experience: "our personal histories and cultural contexts affect the way we understand automatically shared feelings."[36] The absurdity and unfamiliarity of the situation and the context of the patient's pain prohibit readers' empathetic attempt at vicariously imagining themselves in his shoes. Nevertheless readers (including myself) continue to read the episode and wait for the next one to unfold. Despite the absence of mind reading and empathy, the *Dr. P Series* still provokes a strong desire for narrative.

In other words, what happens in GG's episode is at odds with how, according to cognitive literary scholars, narrative operates. The popularity of the episode, however, is a clear indication that an absence of readable minds and empathy can still create a narrative environment that is highly engaging and entertaining, and narrative can be incomprehensible, unpleasant, and amusing simultaneously. Of course, it is biologically possible for people to feel mixed, contradicting feelings concurrently, as opposite feelings are "at best represented by two unipolar dimensions" rather than by a single bipolar dimension—more simply put, different parts of our brain activate feelings of opposite natures, pleasure and displeasure, for instance, while such activation can happen in multiple parts of the brain simultaneously.[37] Recent developments in functional magnetic resonance imaging (fMRI) offer a compelling basis for this two unipolar co-activation approach to opposite feelings: the mapping of the emotional brain through fMRI pictures has shown amygdala as the main neural correlate for fear and other likely negative emotions, whereas happiness and other likely positive emotions usually require prefrontal cortex participation, among other areas.[38]

What is particularly important to note about this co-activation approach to opposite feelings is that the concurrence of mixed feelings is most likely to happen when those who experience such feelings are detached from what they witness, hear, or feel. Scott Hemenover and Ulrich Schimmack conducted an experiment in which participants watched a disgusting-humorous scene from the movie *Pink Flamingos* (1973), in which the main character eats dog feces in a funny manner. Participants in the experiment were divided into two groups. Some were given a role of an insider and read the following instructions:

> Imagine that you are this main character doing, thinking and feeling what this character does. Put yourself in the frame of mind so that you are responding as you would if it was actually you experiencing the situation as the main character.

Some others, on the other hand, were invited to take a position of an outsider and were asked to read the following: "Imagine you have no connection to what is happening and that what is happening cannot impact you in any way. You are simply observing and reacting the events as they unfold."[39] Participants completed a consent form prior to watching the clip and, after the clip, they answered questionnaires assessing their emotional responses between amusement and disgust on a 5-point scale ranging from 0 (not at all) to 4 (extremely). The result of the experiment shows that those who watched the scene from the protagonist's position (the character who eats the dog feces) reported disgusting feelings, whereas those who took the outsider's position reported mixed feelings of disgust and amusement. The experiment reveals two important findings: that the co-occurrence of conflicting feelings (disgust and amusement, displeasure and pleasure) is indeed possible, and that taking an outsider's point of view enhances the experience of mixed feelings.

Given that avoiding an insider's point of view is the major determining factor in eliciting mixed feelings in viewers and entertaining them with what can be potentially unpleasant and aversive, then the absence of readable minds and character identification are key to the success of the *Dr. P Series*. It helps readers to more readily take the third-person outsider perspective rather than the first-person, and to thereby avoid "trespass[ing] the fragile boundary that separates pleasure from pain."[40] Being an observer, those readers, while noticing the pain that the patient character is experiencing, can continue to be entertained by the absurd and aversive narrative situation. Of course, unreadable minds can encourage readers to more actively step into the narrative and take the first-person perspective. For instance, Porter Abbott, in "Unreadable Minds and the Captive Reader," outlines three types of default reading positions in fiction with unreadable minds. Namely, characters who appear to be unreadable can (1) be stereotyped by others, (2) invite a symbolic reading, or (3) function in the characterization of another. In other words, the unreadable mind can be adopted in fiction for specific rhetorical purposes for the author and offer a crucial interpretive strategy through which readers make sense of the narrative. The obscure copyist, Bartleby, in Herman Melville's "Bartleby the Scrivener," is the center of the narrative while the narrator, the lawyer who employs Bartleby, attempts to penetrate Bartleby's inscrutability. As readers take the narrator's perspective, they also join the effort to make Bartleby's unreadable mind readable. In the process of doing so, Bartleby operates "as a catalyst in the drama of non-reading, with the focus on the captive reader [that is, the narrator] as he copes with the unreadable."[41] Bartleby also brings out the lawyer's character and helps thematize and symbolize the dehumanizing business environment of modern society. Rather than observing the unreadable mind from a distance, readers of "Bartleby the Scrivener" deeply engage with it and make sense of it.

This, however, is not what happens in the *Dr. P Series*. In the case of "Bartleby the Scrivener," the ways in which Bartleby's unreadable mind works are in line with how poetic language, as conceptualized by Viktor Shklovsky, defamiliarizes readers. According to Shklovsky, poetic language differs from prosaic language because its fundamental function as a formal device and technique is to make the usual unusual, to interrupt readers' automatic perceptual activities, thereby reforming, renewing, and re-intensifying their perceptions.[42] The poetic devices of defamiliarization, however, "operate through time." Stefan Iversen points out that although they halt, disrupt, and delay readers' perception, in most cases "this stalling functions mainly as a delay, as a bridge to be crossed or a cognitive burden to overcome."[43] Likewise, although frustrating the narrator's (and hence readers') attempts at habitual mind reading, Bartleby's inscrutability is resolved through the default reading strategies that Abbott outlines, adding to and ultimately completing readers' interpretive endeavors. By contrast, the unreadable fictional minds in *Dr. P Series* operate more as a device for "permanent defamiliarization," leading to what Iversen calls the "perpetual unrecognizability."[44] Whereas the process of stereotyping and symbolizing requires a certain degree of familiarity for association, the absurd and incoherent nature of Dr. P's action only further displaces both Dr. P and the patient from a recognizable narrative situation (doctor–patient relationship). As a result, readers are precluded from categorizing or symbolizing the characters and the narrative. Although the patient is puzzled by Dr. P's action and the motive behind it, Dr. P's unreadable mind does not work as "a catalyst in a drama of non-reading," either.[45] Like any webtoon, each episode of *Dr. P Series* is brief and lacks any sustained interaction between the two characters. In other words, each episode ends before the defamiliarization (unreadability) could be crossed and overcome—there is literally no space or time for the unreadability to become a catalyst and to invite readers to engage with it and make sense of it. Rather, the unrecognizability of Dr. P's action and the patient's experience becomes perpetual.

This "perpetual unrecognizability," nevertheless, enables readers to view the narrative with a degree of ease, and it frees them from the violence used in the narrative and from its ethical implications. Precisely because readers give up on Dr. P and the patient as being plausible, readable characters, Dr. P's action and the patient's pain become benign. Readers are released from the burden of ethically evaluating Dr. P and empathizing with the patient. Consequently, readers more readily take on the third-person outsider perspective and, from a safe distance, comfortably observe what is quite aversive and unpleasant. The digitally mediated narrative environment of the webtoon further helps maintain this comfortable distancing. The mediality of webtoon may be best understood in its relation to print comics, whose form webtoon (or any digital comics) has adopted, re-mediated, digitalized, and, in cases of more experimental motion webtoon, animated. Borrowing Scott McCloud's term "infinite canvas," comics scholar Jakob Dittmar argues that the "lack of any printed page [of digital comics]" leads to "an end of conventional narrations and dramaturgical necessities."[46] Furthermore, digital comics' lack of a printed page makes necessary a new panel delivery system. Whereas "[t]he interruption of the continuous flow of reading and the necessity to turn a page can be understood as a technical condition brought on by print," in digital comics, the act of clicking and dragging replaces the act of turning a page, giving both the authors and readers of digital comics more freedom and flexibility from "the physical condition that [the print comic] imposes."[47]

Similarly, readers of *Dr. P Series* are less restricted by "the repetitive beat of the page turn"[48] of the print comics medium and relatively freer from the complexity and ambiguity that print comics' medial structure imposes—including, for instance, the gutter. In *Understanding Comics*, McCloud explains *gutter* as the empty space between the panels that plays "host to much of the magic and mystery that are at the very heart of comics."[49] Whereas comics panels "fracture both time and space, offering a jagged, staccato rhythm of unconnected moments,"[50] the gutter allows readers to take two separate images and connect them to mentally construct a continuous, unified reality. Many comics artists deliberately complicate this mental process for readers for different aesthetic, thematic, and cognitive purposes. For example, they sometimes fill the gutter with different images and even colors, while some others might merge the gutter into the panels ("bleeding"). The various techniques used to reshape the gutter space in comics add complexity and ambiguity to readers' narrative experience, often in productive and enriching ways. The gutter in the *Dr. P Series*, however, eliminates complexity and ambiguity by functioning primarily and simply as a dividing border between the panels. Throughout the episode, each panel is consistently separately by straight black lines. Rather than hosting "the magic and mystery," the gutter in *Dr. P Series* expedites and simplifies the readers' mental processes of creating a continuous, unified reality no matter how absurd that reality may appear.

Likewise, the vertical, top-down arrangement of the panels in the webtoon preempts any ambiguity of complex page layout and panel display. All readers have to do is to automatically and habitually keep on scrolling down the screen and read from top to bottom. Such simplicity and straightforwardedness of the mode of reading that *Dr. P Series*'s digital mediality affords may indeed induce some strong, passionate responses from "true comic fans": "For true comic fans, digital comics aren't going to replace printed traditional ones anytime soon ... There's an elegance to holding a book in your hands ... the activity [of reading digital comics] cheapens the value of their property."[51] Digital comics' lack of "elegance," which supposedly "cheapens" the value of comics, in fact adds more value to readers' narrative experience with the *Dr. P Series*. While the violence and overall unreadability of the episode might add anxiety and discomfort to readers, the webtoon's simple panel delivery system—the easy clicking and dragging—in general renders readers' physical reading experience a lot less intense and complicated. Readers view and could possibly apprehend the violence and pain that the patient undergoes, but the ways in which the comics are structured and mediated lessen the readers' burden of becoming an actual part of the making of this narrative world. Simply put, readers can take it easy and just click and drag without thinking much. In this context, what Yon-sue Choi, a part-time office worker in Korea, says about why she reads webtoon is quite insightful:

> With a smartphone, I can view webtoons anywhere and anytime, be it on the road, during lunch or after a long meeting. All I need to do is click the screen and scroll down. How much more convenient could it get?[52]

With such convenience and comfort of reading, readers of the *Dr. P Series* can keep enough distance from what really happens in the panels and therefore make sure not to direct any unpleasant condition of the narrative toward themselves.

A popular culture critic, Myungsuk Lee, explains that the wide popularity of bad-taste webtoon in Korea is indicative of the frustration and distress that young Koreans experience living in a perfection-driven competitive Korean society.[53] While the society is hungry for what is right and perfect, bad-taste webtoons are incoherently put together, use wrong images and language without shame, and are drawn sketchily with indelicate and hasty lines. All these "bad" elements, however, enable bad-taste webtoons to defy higher social and cultural standards and expectations without having any didactic message about these standards. Readers of bad-taste webtoons are free to release themselves from the burden of having to be always right and perfect and think deeply of what they see and feel. Similarly, in an interview GG once said,

> I do not want my readers to think too deeply about what happens in my webtoons and try to make sense of the characters' actions and minds, because they are not supposed make any sense. I simply want my readers to empty their minds and enjoy the unrealistic, incoherent, and messy [fictional] world as depicted in my webtoons.[54]

When we can abandon the impulse to always read and make sense of the minds of characters in the real and fictional worlds, then we can fully become the captive reader of even the unpleasant, which no longer will be unpleasant.

Encountered: digital narrative and embodied and experiential reading

With its highly experimental and interactive nature and the ways in which it demands its readers to move beyond the position of an observer and virtually join the fictional world as active storyworld participants, *Encountered* differs from the *Dr. P Series*. First published in 2017, *Encountered* is a collaborative project between Naver and popular webtoon artist Ha-Il Kwon, a project that fully utilizes affordances of digital interactive media and facial-recognition and machine-learning technologies. In *Encountered*, a high school love story, the webtoon is shown from the viewpoint of the reader himself/herself and invites readers to step into the fictional world as one of the characters of the narrative. My discussion of *Encountered* centers on the immersive and embodied reading experience that the webtoon, with its digital properties, makes possible for its readers. Specifically, I focus on the ways in which *Encountered* motivates its readers' projection into the storyworld and how this projection leads to readers' spatial and perspectival immersion, which is more embodied and bodily than mentally simulated.

Literary scholars have considered for a long time the relationship between narrative comprehension and narrative immersion. The central questions: How do readers engage with fictional worlds and imaginatively project themselves into these worlds? What are the elements of narrative facilitating such fictional projections and the construction of storyworlds? These worlds are "mental models of who did what to and with whom, when, where, why, and in what fashion in the world to which recipients relocate."[55] David Herman, in "Narrative Theory and the Intentional Stance," explains that readers rely on deictic and referential features, the "world-building elements," to construct a mental model of the world evoked by a text, while these features illuminate "the cognitive reorientation required for an interpreter's successful relocation to a narrative world."[56] Similarly, Marie Laure-Ryan posits that narrative recipients re-orient themselves from the real world that they live in to the worlds constructed by narrative, doing so by "project[ing] upon these worlds everything [they] know about reality, [making] only the adjustments dictated by the text."[57] Kendall Walton calls this process of mental adjustment "the reality principle" and explains that when a text includes an object "that exists in reality, all the real-world properties of this object can be imported into the storyworld unless explicitly contradicted by the text."[58] All these mental processes and imaginations lead to a construction of storyworlds. Readers, depending on how immersed they are in their narrative experience, either relocate to or stay away from these worlds.

Although these approaches are useful to understand how readers simulate and are transported into fictional worlds, their interest clearly is in the mental processes involved in the fictional projection, thereby overlooking how the reader's body also contributes to blending the real world with the fictional world. Indeed, Marco Caracciolo, in "The Reader's Virtual Body," argues that although the mental simulation-oriented approaches are suggestive, "meant to be understood in a metaphorical manner" and, hence, "blunt their effect." In his view, simulation and mental imagery are deeply anchored in readers' real body, as "even when reader is required to make a 'deictic shift,' the reader brings along a virtual counterpart of his or her real body."[59]

In conclusion, our cognitive potential to simulate fictional worlds and be transported into these worlds can be unleashed more fully "only when we regard them as describing something that virtually happens to our own bodies."[60] The different degrees of experientiality that readers feel in different narrative texts, then, can be understood based on the different degrees of embodiedness realized in narratives, and how they allow for readers' bodily access (albeit virtual) to the fictional world. In this regard, it is important to consider how authors encode readers' bodily presence in their narratives by deploying and implementing certain narrative cues designed to create the effect of moving readers' bodies into the fictional world. Furthermore, given my focus on the interactive webtoon, we have to ask what additional and new affordances webtoon's digital medium provides (narrative and technological) to help actualize more readily and effectively the transfer of readers' virtual bodies into the fictional space.

At first, there is nothing so unusual about *Encounter*'s first episode. It is a teen romance set in a high school and revolves around the female protagonist, Joora, and the male protagonist, Sung-joon. Upon the webtoon's opening, and as readers scroll down the screen of their digital devices, light pastel colors fill each panel and give readers a sense of lightness and cheerfulness (like any other romance webtoon). This familiarity is interrupted, however, when the webtoon starts projecting readers' thoughts into the narrative in blue stand-alone letters unbounded by thought balloons: "Well, this looks like a new webtoon uploaded recently. Wait, how and why am I reading my own thoughts and why do they appear inside this fictional world? … At any rate, why is this episode not progressing as quickly? Isn't now the right moment to show inside the classroom and how the two main characters build up their relationship?"[61]

Right after these captions, blurred images of a school and hallways inside the school follow, and the episode transitions to a classroom within which Joora and Sung-joon are now placed. The progression of the episode indicates it is paced in order to reflect thoughts and expectations of the projected imaginary reader. The success of such narrative construction and progression depends, of course, on whether readers are immersed enough in the narrative to take this imaginary reader position and identify with the thoughts being projected in the fictional world, believing that their thoughts can indeed be part of the narrative that they view, and can determine its due course.

Without doubt, the best way to immerse readers into the narrative space is to actually position them inside that space, if that is possible at all. M. Angeles Martinez in "Storyworld Possible Selves and Narrative Immersion," draws particular attention to the linguistic organization of narrative discourse, such as the use of doubly deictic "You" and generic "One," to examine how readers may become immersed in storyworlds. What is especially relevant is Martinez's discussion of "implicit senser in passive-voice mental processes": "The use of the passive voice with mental transitivity processes—process of thinking, feeling, and perceiving—provides an empty intra-diegetic slot that the reader may feel tempted to occupy."[62] Mental processes in fictional narratives usually involve a focalizer as senser. According to Martinez, when this senser entity is only implicitly marked inside a fictional world (the generic "one" as senser, for instance), readers may become more actively involved and immersed in narrative, as they are more likely to enter the "empty intra-diegetic slot" and take up the senser position. In other words, while readers are always encouraged to simulate narrative space and cognitively reorient themselves from the real world to the fictional world, this repositioning happens more effectively and readily when it is triggered by a fictional entity that is less full-fledged and, hence, general enough for any reader to identify with. Caracciolo echoes this idea by saying that while "the fictionally actual bodies into which readers are invited to project themselves" can belong to any character, less-specified characters, such as an unnamed and unspecifiable visitor or traveler, "allow for the highest degree of fictionalization of the reader's virtual body, even higher than full-blown characters."[63]

All of these, however, are indicative of the challenge that the traditional print medium, with its intrinsic properties, imposes on narrative and narrative recipients. It is of course nearly impossible for any print text to present a full-blown fictional character with specific physical, emotional, psychological, and physiological traits, and to invite widely different readers from all corners of life to equally identify with him/her. *Encounter*'s digital medium, however, helps overcome this impossibility and encodes in the narrative an explicit and fully specified virtual position that any reader may be tempted to occupy and identify with. For instance, soon after the episode transitions to the classroom, a panel with an empty chair appears and draws readers' attention. This panel is then followed by a character who directly faces readers and asks, "What is your name?" In the next panel, readers are presented with an empty box where readers, using their own keyboards, are asked to type in their real names. Once the name is typed in, the same character, who asked for the name in the first place, starts calling readers by their real names. This projection of individual readers' real names into the fictional world effectively creates an explicit, fully blown intra-diegetic slot that any reader curious enough to type in his/her name may gladly and bodily take on. The empty chair in the panel is, hence, occupied by those readers.

The webtoon's digital medium takes further the idea of actualizing readers' virtual body in the narrative space by asking readers to take a selfie using the camera installed in their digital devices. Once readers take a selfie, webtoon's facial-recognition technology converts the picture into a drawing, constructing and implementing a character with facial traits that closely resemble those of the real people reading the webtoon. This character, the reader stand-in, starts interacting with other (truly) fictional characters in the episode. As readers witness themselves (virtually) turning into a character in the narrative, they, with their virtual body fictionalized in the webtoon, step into the narrative world, occupy the position explicitly available for them, and blend with the other characters. The construction of virtual bodies in the fictional space, into which readers project themselves, can of course happen in more traditional print narratives and makes possible embodied narrative experience for readers. In print narratives, however, this experience is by default vicarious and simulated mentally, as there always is an ontological difference between the real world and the fictional world that can never be completely overcome. Using facial-recognition and machine-learning technologies, *Encountered* makes a meaningful attempt to lessen the degree of this ontological divergence between the real and fictional worlds and maximize readers' sense of embodiedness and experientiality in narrative.

The increased sense of experientiality in *Encountered* is also attributable to the webtoon's use of augmented reality and a 360-degree panorama view. In her study of the role of vision in embodied, enactive approaches to perception, Karin Kukkonen, referring to Kevin O'Regan and Alva Noe's 2001 article, defines vision as "a mode of exploration of the world that is mediated by knowledge of what we call sensorimotor contingencies."[64] That is, in order to make sense of a given environment, "[o]ur bodies relate to interaction potentials of our environment and, as our sensorimotor system gives us information about what it would be like to interact with this environment, we perceive it in these terms."[65] Our eyes take a significant role in allowing for this strongly embodied sense of what we perceive because we process the information on the retina "by relating it to the sensorimotor contingencies of interacting with the world" and making sense of the world "in terms of how it is 'available' to us."[66] The availability of the represented world in *Encountered* increases due to the "elimination of page breaks and paper sizes"[67] and to the technologies used in the webtoon. For instance, the image of an empty chair mentioned earlier transitions to a 360-degree view of the classroom, granting readers access to the spaces and characters—access that would otherwise have been left unnoticed. As readers browse their 360-degree surroundings and view all four corners of the classroom, more elements of the represented environment become available to their vision. Readers, through their retina, then filter and process this information and make sense of it by, as quoted above, "relating it to the sensorimotor contingencies of interacting with the world." Simply put, as readers are able to see and access more elements of "the [fictional] world's encyclopedia,"[68] readers' sensorimotor system is further simulated in such a way that the interaction potential of the given environment increases, leading to the heightened level of narrative experientiality. Readers see, feel, experience, and comprehend more within the expanded spatial make-up of the narrative.

Readers' interaction with the represented environment, however, matters only if readers find meaning, value, and relevance in that space and are motivated enough to explore it further. After all, as Marie-Laure Ryan, in her study of the ways in which readers simulate spatial make-up of storyworlds, says, "people read for the plot and not for the map."[69] In her investigation of interactive computer games and the role of plot in these games, Ryan also notes that

> [a] car chase by itself may be visually stunning, but it only becomes narratively meaningful if the chaser and the chasee have reasons to behave the way they do ... To rival the narrative richness of other media, then, a system of interactive storytelling must be able to stage both physical actions that change the fictional world and verbal acts that affect the minds of its inhabitants and motivate them to take action.[70]

In this regard, readers' embodied narrative experience in *Encountered* is more fully complete only if their bodily interaction with and involvement in the narrative space are simultaneously compelled by the "verbal acts" of the narrative, which can motivate and give meaning to readers' physical/bodily relationship with the narrative.

In fact, this is exactly what happens to readers in *Encountered*. Readers not only perceive, and thereby simulate and experience, the given environment through the activation of their sensorimotor systems (mirror neuron and motor resonance, for instance), but they also build up a meaningful relationship with one of the characters of the webtoon, Younghee, an outcast bullied by her classmates. Younghee is the very character who calls readers by their names and interacts with the reader as stand-in. She even shares eye contact with readers by blinking when readers blink. Younghee invites readers into her perspective, evokes empathetic feelings in readers' minds, and becomes dependent upon readers and their involvement in the narrative: the more deeply involved readers are in the narrative and in their relationship with Youngee, the happier this lone character becomes. In other words, while *Encountered*'s digitally mediated narrative environment affords readers bodily involvement and engagement with the webtoon, Younghee's presence and the verbal acts that it elicits are what make readers' bodily reaction to the narrative more meaningful and relevant. To borrow Ryan's words, readers read not only for the embodied experientiality, but for the story that shapes this experientiality in specific ways and for specific effects.

Readers, by interacting with Younghee and caring for her through the body of their virtual self in the fictional world, are able to give more agency to her character and also influence her situation and action in the webtoon. Readers can even bring Younghee into the real world their actual body belongs to. Using the camera of their digital device, readers can project Younghee (as a cut-out figure) against the view of the real world that their camera captures. Readers make possible the blending of the two ontologically separate worlds, "the transfer of meanings between the fictional world and the real world."[71] Readers' relationship with Younghee constitutes a parallel plot in *Encountered* and, as Ryan says, "rivals the narrative richness of [webtoon's digital medium]," consequently rendering the stunning interactive technologies and the visual of the webtoon more suggestive, consequential, and relevant.

McCloud, in *Reinventing Comics*, has called digital comics "an infinite canvas":

> The page is an artifact of print, no more intrinsic to comics than staples or [I]ndia ink. Once released from that box, some will take the shape of the box with them but gradually comics creators will stretch their limbs and start to explore the design opportunities of an infinite canvas.[72]

The two webtoons analyzed in this chapter show exactly how comics creators are "stretch[ing] their limbs" in order to explore the infinite possibilities that the shift of the medium (from print to the digital) has opened up for them. The close reading of the two webtoons has also shown exactly how these possibilities can be implemented in the narrative for specific cognitive, emotional, and bodily effects on readers. Moreover, this chapter has allowed for more careful consideration of the interconnectivity and interdependence between the old and new media in the context of media convergence and remediation, and how the different affordances of each medium contribute to constructing narrative and entertainment experiences that productively challenge how and why we read, view, and interact with narrative. In this regard, Korean webtoons and their popularity and spread offer scholars of a wide range of disciplines the very "infinite canvas" to explore.

Notes

1 Portions of this chapter appeared in Hyesu Park, "Joy of Ugly Feelings: Korean 'Bad Taste' Webtoons as a Case Study," *Studies in 20th & 21st Century Literature* 42, no. 1 (2017): 1–14. http://doi.org/10.4148/2334-4415.1960.

"Manga," *Wikipedia*, accessed March 2, 2020, https://en.wikipedia.org/wiki/Manga.
2 "Manhwa," *Wikipedia*, accessed March 2, 2020, https://en.wikipedia.org/wiki/Manhwa.
3 Woo-young Lee, "Korean Webtoons Make Big Strides in Global Comics Market," *The Korean Herald*, August 16, 2016, www.koreaherald.com/view.php?ud=20160816000430.
4 Joo-Hee Hong and Eun-Soo Jin, "Webtoons Aim to Draw in More Overseas Readers," *Korea JoongAng Daily*, January 26, 2015, https://koreajoongangdaily.joins.com/news/article/Article.aspx?aid=3000152.
5 Gi-Hyun Yoon, "Examining Korean Webtoons through Statistics," *The Korean Manhwa Contents Agency*, June 27, 2014, http://dml.komacon.kr/webzine/normal/2507. [my trans.]
6 See Dal Yong Jin, "Digital Convergence of Korea's Webtoons: Transmedia Storytelling," *Communication Research and Practice* 1, no. 3 (2015): 193–209 and Kee-Bom Nam, Won-Ho Jang, and Jung-Eun Song, "The Impact of Spread of Webtoon on the Development of Hallyu: The Case Study of Indonesia," *The Academic Association for Korean Entertainment Industry* (2014): 357–367, doi: 10.21184/jkeia.2014.06.8.2.357. [my trans].
7 Dafna Zur, "Modern Korean Literature and Cultural Identity in a Pre- and Post-Colonial Digital Age," in *Routledge Handbook of Korean Culture and Society*, ed. Youna Kim (New York: Routledge, 2016), 193–205.
8 See Lisa Zunshine, *Getting Inside Your Head: What Cognitive Science Can Tell Us About Popular Culture* (Baltimore: Johns Hopkins University Press, 2012).
9 Henry Jenkins, "Transmedia 202: Further Reflections," *Confession of an Aca-Fan*, July 31, 2011, http://henryjenkins.org/blog/2011/08/defining_transmedia_further_re.html.
10 Adam Rowe, "Report: Film Adaptations of Books Earn 53% More at The Worldwide Box Office, *Forbes*, July 11, 2018, www.forbes.com/sites/adamrowe1/2018/07/11/why-book-based-films-earn-53-more-at-the-worldwide-box-office/#283f9a5c306f.
11 Marshall McLuhan, *Essential McLuhan*, ed. Eric McLuhan and Frank Zingrone (New York: Basic Books, 1996), 188.
12 Jenkins, "Transmedia."
13 Marie-Laure Ryan, "Introduction," in *Narrative across Media: The Languages of Storytelling*, ed. Marie-Laure Ryan (Lincoln: University of Nebraska Press, 2004), 31.
14 Jin, "Digital," 196.
15 Ibid., 199.
16 "S. Korea Tops Smartphone Penetration Rate in 2018: Report," *Yonhap News*, February 6, 2019, https://en.yna.co.kr/view/AEN20190206001200325.
17 Lee, "Korean Webtoons."
18 Zur, "Modern Korean," 8.

19 Fernando Duarte, "Which Country Works the Longest Hours?," *BBC News*, accessed March 8, 2020, www.bbc.com/worklife/article/20180504-which-country-works-the-longest-hours.
20 Jo-young Sohn, "Korean Webtoons Going Global," *The Korean Herald*, May 25, 2014, www.koreaherald.com/view.php?ud=20140525000452.
21 Jenkins, "Transmedia."
22 Marue-Laure Ryan, "Will New Media Produce New Narratives?" in *Narrative across Media: The Languages of Storytelling*, ed. Marie-Laure Ryan (Lincoln: University of Nebraska Press, 2004), 337.
23 Ryan, "Introduction," 17.
24 Lee, "Korean Webtoons."
25 For the official website of K-Webtoon, see www.k-webtoon.kr/contents/siteMain.do?srch_mu_lang=CDIDX00023.
26 Nam, Jang, and Song, "The Impact," 359.
27 Porter Abbott, "Unreadable Minds and the Captive Reader," *Style* 42, no. 4 (2008): 448.
28 Lisa Zunshine, *Why We Read Fiction: Theory of Mind and the Novel* (Columbus: Ohio State University Press, 2006), 6.
29 Lisa Zunshine, "Why We Read Fiction," *Skeptical Inquirer* 30, no. 6 (2006): 30.
30 Zunshine, *Theory*, 275.
31 Suzanne Keen, "A Theory of Narrative Empathy," *Narrative* 14, no. 3 (2006): 208.
32 dcinside, www.dcinside.com.
33 Geun-woo Wee, "The Origin of Bad Taste Webtoon: It Is Okay to Feel Uncomfortable," *Hangyurae*, October 4, 2013, www.hani.co.kr/arti/culture/movie/605822.html. [my trans.]
34 Gyui Gyui (GG). "Episode 1," *Dr. P Series*, accessed April 25, 2020, http://m.cafe.naver.com/hojin31/634.
35 Jung-hyun Hwang, "After Makjang Dramas Comes Bad Taste Webtoon," *Media today*, April 11, 2010, www.mediatoday.co.kr/news/articleView.html?mod=news&act=articleView&idxno=87360. [my trans.]
36 Suzanne Keen, "A Theory of Narrative Empathy," *Narrative* 14, no. 3 (2006): 209.
37 Ulrich Schimmack, "Pleasure, Displeasure, and Mixed Feelings: Are Semantic Opposites Mutually Exclusive?" *Cognition and Emotion* 15, no. 1 (2001): 82.
38 Eduardo Andrade and Joel Cohen, "On the Consumption of Negative Feelings," *Journal of Consumer Research* 34, no. 3 (2007): 286.
39 Scott Hemenover and Ulrich Schimmack, "That's Disgusting! …, but Very Amusing: Mixed Feelings of Amusement and Disgust," *Cognition and Emotion* 21, no. 5 (2007): 1106.
40 Ryan, "Will New Media," 347.
41 Abbott, "Unreadable," 451.
42 Viktor Shklovsky, *Theory of Prose* (Chicago: Dalkey Archive Press, 1991).

43 Stefan Iversen, "Permanent Defamiliarization as Rhetorical Device; or, How to Let Puppymonkeybaby into Unnatural Narratology," *Style* 50, no. 4 (2016): 459.
44 Ibid., 460.
45 Abbott, "Unreadable," 451.
46 Jakob Dittmar, "Digital Comics," *Scandinavian Journal of Comic Arts* 1, no. 2 (2012): 84.
47 Lukas Wilde, "Distinguishing Mediality: The Problem of Identifying Forms and Features of Digital Comics," *Networking Knowledge* 8, no. 4 (2015): 7.
48 Ibid.
49 Scott McCloud, *Understanding Comics* (New York: Harpers Collins, 1994), 66.
50 Ibid.
51 Jeffrey Kirchoff, "It's Just Not the Same as Print (and It Shouldn't Be): Rethinking the Possibilities of Digital Comics," accessed May 13, 2020, http://tcjournal.org/drupal/print/vol3/kirchoff.
52 Sohn, "Korean Webtoons."
53 Mi-Young Kim, "Bad Taste Webtoons, the Beautiful Catharsis!" *hani.21*, accessed April 3, 2020, http://h21.hani.co.kr/arti/culture/culture_general/ 27079.html.
54 Ibid.
55 David Herman, *Story Logic* (Lincoln: University of Nebraska Press, 2002), 9.
56 David Herman, "Narrative Theory and the Intentional Stance," *Partial Answers: Journal of Literature and the History of Ideas* 6, no. 2 (2008): 250.
57 Marie-Laure Ryan, *Possible Worlds, Artificial Intelligence, and Narrative Theory* (Bloomington: Indiana University Press, 1991), 51.
58 Kendall Walton, *Mimesis as Make-Believe: On the Foundations of the Representational Acts* (Cambridge, MA: Harvard University Press, 1990), 145.
59 Marco Caracciolo, "The Reader's Virtual Body," *Storyworlds* 3 (2011): 119
60 Ibid., 118.
61 Ha-Il Kwon, "Episode 1," *Encountered*, December 11, 2017, https://comic. naver.com/webtoon/detail.nhn?titleId=703634&no=1&weekday=.
62 M. Angeles Martinez, "Storyworld Possible Selves and the Phenomenon of Narrative Immersion: Testing a New Theoretical Construct," *Narrative* 22, no. 1 (2014): 114.
63 Caracciolo, "The Reader's," 122.
64 Karin Kukkonen, "Presence and Prediction: The Embodied Reader's Cascades of Cognition," *Style* 48, no. 3 (2014): 369.
65 Ibid.
66 Ibid.
67 Wilde, "Distinguishing," 7.
68 Lubomir Dolezel, *Heterocosmica: Fiction and Possible Worlds* (Baltimore: Johns Hopkins University Press, 1998), 181.

69 Marie-Laure Ryan, "Cognitive Maps and the Construction of Narrative Space," in *Narrative Theory and the Cognitive Sciences*, ed. David Herman (Stanford: CSLI, 2003), 238.
70 Marie-Laure Ryan, "From Narrative Games to Playable Stories: Toward a Poetics of Interactive Narrative," *Storyworlds* 1 (2009): 48.
71 Caracciolo, "The Reader's," 126.
72 Scott McCloud, *Reinventing Comics* (New York: William Morrow Paperbacks, 2001), 222.

Bibliography

Abbott, Porter. "Unreadable Minds and the Captive Reader." *Style* 42, no. 4 (2008): 448–466.
Andrade, Eduardo and Joel Cohen. "On the Consumption of Negative Feelings." *Journal of Consumer Research* 34, no. 3 (2007): 283–300.
Caracciolo, Marco. "The Reader's Virtual Body." *Storyworlds* 3 (2011): 117–138.
Dolezel, Lubomir. *Heterocosmica: Fiction and Possible Worlds*. Baltimore: Johns Hopkins University Press, 1998.
Dittmar, Jakob. "Digital Comics." *Scandinavian Journal of Comic Arts* 1, no. 2 (2012): 83–91.
Duarte, Fernando. "Which Country Works the Longest Hours?" *BBC News*. Accessed March 8, 2020. www.bbc.com/worklife/article/20180504-which-country-works-the-longest-hours.
Gyui Gyui (GG). "Episode 1." *Dr. P Series*. Accessed April 25, 2020. http://m.cafe.naver.com/hojin31/634.
Hemenover, Scott and Ulrich Schimmack. "That's Disgusting! ..., but Very Amusing: Mixed Feelings of Amusement and Disgust." *Cognition and Emotion* 21, no. 5 (2007): 1102–1113.
Herman, David. *Story Logic*. Lincoln: University of Nebraska Press, 2002.
———. "Narrative Theory and the Intentional Stance." *Partial Answers: Journal of Literature and the History of Ideas* 6, no. 2 (2008): 233–260.
Hong, Joo-Hee and Eun-Soo Jin. "Webtoons Aim to Draw in More Overseas Readers." *Korea JoongAng Daily*. January 26 (2015). https://koreajoongangdaily.joins.com/news/article/Article.aspx?aid=3000152.
Hwang, Jung-hyun. "After Makjang Dramas Comes Bad Taste Webtoon." *Media Today*. April 11 (2010). www.mediatoday.co.kr/news/articleView.html?mod=news&act=articleView&idxno=87360. [my trans.]
Iversen, Stefan. "Permanent Defamiliarization as Rhetorical Device; or, How to Let Puppymonkeybaby into Unnatural Narratology." *Style* 50, no. 4 (2016): 455–462.
Jenkins, Henry. "Transmedia 202: Further Reflections." *Confession of an Aca-Fan*. July 31, 2011. http://henryjenkins.org/blog/2011/08/defining_transmedia_further_re.html.
Jin, Dal Yong. "Digital convergence of Korea's webtoons: transmedia storytelling." *Communication Research and Practice* 1, no. 3 (2015): 193–209.

Keen, Suzanne. "A Theory of Narrative Empathy." *Narrative* 14, no.3 (2006): 207–237.
Kim, Mi-Young. "Bad Taste Webtoons, the Beautiful Catharsis!" *hani.21.* Accessed April 3, 2020. http://h21.hani.co.kr/arti/culture/culture_general/27079.html.
Kirchoff, Jeffrey. "It's Just Not the Same as Print (and It Shouldn't Be): Rethinking the Possibilities of Digital Comics." Accessed May 13, 2020. http://tcjournal.org/drupal/print/vol3/kirchoff.
Kukkonen, Karin. "Presence and Prediction: The Embodied Reader's Cascades of Cognition." *Style* 48, no. 3 (2014): 367–384.
Kwon, Ha-Il. "Episode 1." *Encountered.* December 11, 2017. https://comic.naver.com/webtoon/detail.nhn?titleId=703634&no=1&weekday=.
Lee, Woo-young. "Korean Webtoons Make Big Strides in Global Comics Market." *The Korean Herald.* August 16 (2016). www.koreaherald.com/view.php?ud=20160816000430.
Martinez, M. Angeles. "Storyworld Possible Selves and the Phenomenon of Narrative Immersion: Testing a New Theoretical Construct." *Narrative* 22, no. 1 (2014): 110–131.
"Manga." *Wikipedia.* Accessed March 2, 2020. https://en.wikipedia.org/wiki/Manga.
"Manhwa." *Wikipedia.* Accessed March 2, 2020. https://en.wikipedia.org/wiki/Manhwa.
McCloud, Scott. *Understanding Comics.* New York: Harpers Collins, 1994.
_____. *Reinventing Comics.* New York: William Morrow Paperbacks, 2001.
McLuhan, Marshall. *Essential McLuhan*, edited by Eric McLuhan and Frank Zingrone. New York: Basic Books, 1996.
Nam, Kee-Bom, Won-Ho Jang, and Jung-Eun Song. "The Impact of Spread of Webtoon on the Development of Hallyu: The Case Study of Indonesia." *The Academic Association for Korean Entertainment Industry* (2014): 357–367. doi: 10.21184/jkeia.2014.06.8.2.357. [my trans.]
Park. Hyesu. "Joy of Ugly Feelings: Korean 'Bad Taste' Webtoons as a Case Study." *Studies in 20th & 21st Century Literature* 42, no. 1 (2017): 1–14. http://doi.org/10.4148/2334-4415.1960.
Rowe, Adam. "Report: Film Adaptations of Books Earn 53% More at the Worldwide Box Office." *Forbes.* July 11 (2018). www.forbes.com/sites/adamrowe1/2018/07/11/why-book-based-films-earn-53-more-at-the-worldwide-box-office/#283f9a5c306f.
Ryan, Marie-Laure. *Possible Worlds, Artificial Intelligence, and Narrative Theory.* Bloomington: Indiana University Press, 1991.
_____. "Cognitive Maps and the Construction of Narrative Space." In *Narrative Theory and the Cognitive Sciences*, edited by David Herman, 214–242. Stanford: CSLI, 2003.
_____. "Introduction." In *Narrative across Media: The Languages of Storytelling*, edited by Marie-Laure Ryan, 1–40. Lincoln: University of Nebraska Press, 2004.

———. "Will New Media Produce New Narratives?" In *Narrative across Media: The Languages of Storytelling*, edited by Marie-Laure Ryan, 337–359. Lincoln: University of Nebraska Press, 2004.

———. "From Narrative Games to Playable Stories: Toward a Poetics of Interactive Narrative." *Storyworlds* 1 (2009): 43–59.

"S. Korea Tops Smartphone Penetration Rate in 2018: Report." *Yonhap News*. February 6 (2019). https://en.yna.co.kr/view/AEN20190206001200325.

Sohn, Jo-young. "Korean Webtoons Going Global." *The Korean Herald*. May 25 (2014). www.koreaherald.com/view.php?ud=20140525000452.

Schimmack, Ulrich. "Pleasure, Displeasure, and Mixed Feelings: Are Semantic Opposites Mutually Exclusive?" *Cognition and Emotion* 15, no. 1 (2001): 81–97.

Shklovsky, Viktor. *Theory of Prose*. Chicago: Dalkey Archive Press, 1991.

Walton, Kendall. *Mimesis as Make-Believe: On the Foundations of the Representational Acts*. Cambridge, MA: Harvard University Press, 1990.

Wee, Geun-woo. "The Origin of Bad Taste Webtoon: It Is Okay to Feel Uncomfortable." *Hangyurae*. October 4 (2013). www.hani.co.kr/arti/culture/movie/605822.html. [my trans.]

Wilde, Lukas. "Distinguishing Mediality: The Problem of Identifying Forms and Features of Digital Comics." *Networking Knowledge* 8, no. 4 (2015): 1–14.

Yoon, Gi-Hyun. "Examining Korean Webtoons Through Statistics." *The Korean Manhwa Contents Agency*. June 27 (2014). http://dml.komacon.kr/webzine/normal/2507. [my trans.]

Zunshine, Lisa. *Getting Inside Your Head: What Cognitive Science Can Tell Us About Popular Culture*. Baltimore: Johns Hopkins University Press, 2012.

Zur, Dafna. "Modern Korean Literature and Cultural Identity in a Pre- and Post-Colonial Digital Age." In *Routledge Handbook of Korean Culture and Society*, edited by Youna Kim, 193–205. New York: Routledge, 2016.

Zunshine, Lisa. *Why We Read Fiction: Theory of Mind and the Novel*. Columbus: Ohio State University Press, 2006.

Zunshine, Lisa. "Why We Read Fiction." *Skeptical Inquirer* 30, no. 6 (2006): 29–33.

3 Korean mukbang wave

Making sense of eating and broadcasting and its techno-mediated narrative environment

This chapter explores another recent media trend in South Korea (hereafter Korea), *mukbang*. Mukbang, meaning in Korean, "eating and broadcasting," is an online audiovisual broadcast in which a host eats food in front of a camera while talking to his/her viewers or remaining silent, without any verbal communication. Mukbang became popular in Korea in the late 2000s by broadcast jockeys (BJs) who started livestreaming their shows, wherein they consume large meals while using online live streaming platforms such as Afreeca TV or YouTube. Some of these shows have an online chat box and allow viewers to directly interact with BJs, making possible the real-time communication between host and viewers. My discussion of mukbang in this chapter is a revisit to my earlier study of mukbang in "Media, Narrative, and Culture: Narrativizing and Contextualizing Mukbang Shows," included in *Media Culture in Transnational Asia: Convergences and Divergences*, an anthology I edited in 2020.[1] My focus in that chapter was on two kinds of mukbang shows: an interactive show with chat box, and a silent show without any direct participation from viewers. I investigated the ways in which silent mukbang shows help stimulate mental models of storyworlds in spite of their limited range of narrative cues. In the case of interactive mukbang shows, I focused on how the specific cultural elements of South Korea, along with the technical and narratological affordances of digital media, allow viewers of mukbang to make sense of, and even take pleasure in, hosts consuming overly large amounts of food in a strikingly self-abusive manner.

In this chapter, my interest lies specifically in an interactive mukbang show as I consider deeply how the techno-mediated narrative environment of the show informs and even subverts the usual hierarchical dynamics and relationships between narrative/media producer and consumer in such a way that narrative recipients come to take on a more active role, participating in and contributing to the meaning-making process. As in the previous two chapters, I turn to the existing narratological model in order to make sense of the production and consumption of mukbang, and how mukbang as a cultural and media product for communication and expression engages viewers. However, the core of current narrative theory is still predominantly concerned with narrative/narrative text wherein verbal structures and content are fixed and deemed unconditional. In using interactive new media situated specifically within a Korean context as a site for narrative investigation, then, my goal is to suggest a move toward media and narrative studies that are culturally informed and fluidly respond to the specificities of time and place. Importantly, too, I present a study whose focus reflects not only the text[2] (as a pre-structured, fixed artifact) produced and consumed, but "textual features of the object of analysis that involve textual conditions"[3] that are simultaneously technical, semiotic, cultural, psychological, and behavioral.

Narrative or narrative text, as Marie-Laurie Ryan puts it, can be defined as "one that brings a world to the mind (setting) and populates it with intelligent agents (characters)."[4] Precisely because this "logico-semantic characterization of narrative is sufficiently abstract to be regarded as a cognitive universal but flexible enough to tolerate a wide range of variations,"[5] narrative can take numerous different forms, while its meaning can be shaped and filtered specifically by these forms. Different media with their varying forms and configurations, hence, urge new models for narrative expression, communication, and interpretation that can account for the very flexibility of narrative/narrative text that Ryan speaks of. Digital media, in particular that using an Internet platform, have drastically changed how narrative or narrative text can be produced, consumed, and disseminated. This is because, among other things, digital media are reactive and interactive, are equipped with multiple sensory and semiotic channels, and allow for networking among media producers and users across space and time.[6] Understanding these digital properties and their narratological and communicative impacts and consequences—which I do in this chapter by using BJ Changhyun's interactive mukbang show as a case study—will help make sense of the why and how of mukbang in Korea, "the strange phenomenon trending throughout the country."[7]

Korea as a cultural site for mukbang and mukbang's global spread

There are a few common and standard features of mukbang shows. Most mukbang hosts usually eat so-called "junk food," including instant noodles, fried chicken, and a wide range of desserts, to name a few. They also consume abnormally large amounts of food. A typical mukbang episode begins with a host enumerating food items placed before him or her on a table, either large quantities of a single item or five or six (or even more) double-portion dishes. Although mukbang is a recent, "strange" occurrence, food television, whose format Korean mukbang has adapted and transformed, has been a long-standing phenomenon globally. In the United States, for instance, there were already several cable channels dedicated to food and cooking by the mid 1940s, including the 1946 cooking show by famous chef James Beard.[8] There are numerous ways to theorize the global popularity of cooking/food shows, but Pauline Adema finds the key to the success of American food television in the ambiguity of contemporary American society—an ambiguity that involves the desire for "clear and solid values to live by" coexisting with the desire "to embrace the limitless possibilities of modern life and experience that obliterates all values."[9] Food and cooking shows enable viewers to maintain a delicate balance between these two opposing kinds of desire by incorporating "the vicarious pleasures of watching someone else cook and eat; the emulsion of entertainment and cooking; the jumbling of traditional gender roles; and the ambivalence toward cultural standards of body, consumption, and health."[10] Viewers of food television can have endless options of all kinds of scrumptious food and vicariously enjoy them from the privacy and comfort of their own home while not having to worry about the consequences of excessive eating.

Similarly, the irony of contemporary Korean society can explain the popularity of interactive mukbang shows in Korea, as these shows confound desires for individualism and connection on the one hand and issues of control and excess on the other hand. For instance, it is mostly those who live by themselves who subscribe to mukbang channels and programs in Korea. In the era of neo-Confucianism, Asia as a whole has undergone drastic transformations, and Korea is not an exception in this regard. Most notably, individualism, or individualized lifestyle, no longer belongs to Western or British-American society exclusively. Individualism now distinctively characterizes urban lifestyles in Korea. According to the Korean Statistical Information Service's 2017 statistics, one-person households make up 27.2 percent of the more than 20 million households in South Korea.[11] Nevertheless, the sense of oneself as an independent, "freely choosing individual"[12] was never a characteristic of Korean cultural tradition. Consequently, one notices interesting ambivalence and irony in Korea's individualism—a yearning for the emancipatory, Western lifestyle on one hand and a desire for connection and belonging on the other. Mukbang shows powerfully appeal to those viewers who live and dine alone and help them establish, albeit virtually, this very connection that they may be missing in their actual lives. The use of chat box in interactive mukbang is especially important in this regard. Viewers of mukbang not only directly interact with their host by posting their comments, but they also connect to fellow viewers by exchanging their thoughts, feelings, and interests. Consequently, a strong sense of community and empathetic affiliation is established between the host and viewers as well as among viewers.[13] YouTube comments, such as, "I am watching this while eating my lunch!" and "omg I just ordered my food as well, so let's eat together," evidently show how viewers of mukbang watch the shows for emotional connection and virtual togetherness (amidst the absence of physical togetherness).[14] After all, the image of someone dining alone is not an unusual scene to most viewers, and viewers reach out to mukbang shows in order to fill a void in their hearts.

Moreover, the interactive nature of mukbang shows with chat box makes the vicarious consumption of food seem quite literal. Chat box conversations between the mukbang host and viewers show that the dynamics and relationships between them resemble those of role-playing. That is, the mukbang host takes on the role of someone who does the eating for viewers, while viewers occupy a position of a controller who gives instructions to the host about how and what he/she should eat: Can you please drink the soup first? How does the cake taste with chocolate milk? Can you please wrap your meat with the lettuce and eat? Such viewer comments reveal that audiences watch mukbang in order to sate their own cravings for food and vicariously consume it in the specific ways that they would have liked to if they were free from the constraints of control and cultural standards of body and beauty. Of course, anxiety about food consumption is rather universal, especially for women, particularly in some developed nations, and is by no means an exclusively Korean phenomenon. Nevertheless, "lookism," a term used to refer to the attitude of privileging physical attractiveness, is especially widespread and deeply rooted in modern Korean society.[15] According to a 2015 survey by Nielsen Korea, conducted online with 3 million people from 60 different countries, 6 out of 10 Koreans answered that they considered themselves to be overweight, scoring higher (60 percent) than the global average of 49 percent with this opinion. This is striking given that Korea has the lowest overweight rate among all OECD (Organization for Economic Cooperation and Development) nations. It is also notable that one out of two Koreans is regularly on a diet, rigorously controlling his or her daily food consumption.[16] Food anxiety and body dissatisfaction cause many other problems, such as eating disorders and excessive exercise, but more and more people seem to try to vicariously benefit from the comfort and pleasure inherent in food by ingesting media related to food and cooking. Extreme lookism in Korea, coupled with the increase in individualized lifestyle and the ubiquity of mobile devices aided by the world's fastest Internet—which makes possible easy and quick access to any streaming show—facilitates a perfect environment for the production and consumption of mukbang.

Although the specificities of Korean culture, society, and technology have greatly shaped mukbang's birth and growth, the mukbang phenomenon has crossed the national borders and become a global sensation. Although globalization is often considered a mediated Western cultural force, "Asian media have emerged as new players for transnational consumption, changing the dynamics of the media landscape in the region."[17] Asian media are in fact becoming new global cultural forces beyond the region, as the worldwide spread of Korean mukbang signals. American mukbang, inspired by Korean mukbang and started by long-time YouTube user Trisha Paytas, who uploaded her own mukbang video on YouTube in late April 2015, is an example of where Korean media products, strange or not, are changing not only the landscape within the region but also beyond the region. It also proves compellingly that culture and cultural identity, which inform and are informed by media, are no longer restricted by geographical and national boundaries—media and their digital circulation are further reinforcing the adaptive and transformative nature of culture.[18] In fact, mukbang has numerous universal appeals that are not necessarily restricted to Korea only. Dining, after all, has always been inherently social, and the modernization and subsequent isolation of human life have long been global trends. This universal, natural desire to share a meal with good company against the backdrop of isolated modern life has drawn many hosts and viewers on YouTube to mukbang.[19] Some cross-cultural studies on mukbang also report that its global spread can be understood through its sexual aspect, as it facilitates "a sexualized gaze to attractive mukbangers while they are in a somewhat private and vulnerable state (i.e., eating)."[20] Indeed, a cross-cultural study involving 114 Asian and 129 Caucasian participants, who watch mukbang shows regularly, demonstrates that "host attractiveness [is] positively related to attitudes toward mukbang in both samples."[21]

Another element evident in any mukbang broadcast across borders is the use of elaborate and advanced sound equipment designed to maximize food noises—the swallowing, slurping, chewing, and so forth. These vivid food noises create an illusion that helps viewers feel as though someone is dining right next to them, although these noises are likely to provoke an autonomous sensory motor response (ASMR). According to Craig Richard, who has created a website dedicated to the study of ASMR, it can be simulated "during moment of positive, personal attention (the Context) coupled with a gentle voice, touch, sound, and or movement (the Triggers)." The effects of ASMR are quite similar to those of music, as they both induce relaxation, have a strong auditory component, and can foster a physical response: tingles or chills, for instance.[22] In the case of mukbang, the act of eating (and watching it) serves as the context for ASMR while the noises made by mukbang hosts become the triggers that lead to a sensation of sparkling brain tingles that seem to relax and sooth many of the viewers who are drawn to the shows. Of course, mukbang broadcasts are facing increasing criticisms as they could potentially promote self-destructive eating habits and styles and encourage eating disorders, especially for those who watch the show as an alternative to eating and choose to vicariously satisfy their needs for food consumption. These concerns make attempts at understanding the why and how of mukbang all the more relevant and urgent.

Case study: BJ Changhyun, "Roulette Mission Mukbang"

BJ Changhyun is one of the many Korean mukbang hosts who regularly appear on Afreeca TV, and he uploads his recorded livestreams to YouTube for more viewers to watch them retrospectively. These YouTube videos are useful resources for the study of interactivity in mukbang as BJ Changhyun archives all chat messages from his viewers and includes them in his uploads. As my close reading of his video clip will show, the interaction between BJ Changhyun and his viewers is informed by the cultural, social, and psychological elements mentioned earlier in this chapter. However, it is important to note how the host–viewer interaction on his show is also shaped by the techno-mediated narrative environment of mukbang broadcasting. My analysis of BJ Changhyun's show draws particular attention to the relationship between medium and narrative, as well as how this relationship invites new considerations for narrative construction, performance, perception, and dissemination in the context of interactive digital media. After all, as Marie-Laure Ryan points out, "when interactivity is added to the text or the movie, its ability to tell stories, and the stories it can tell, are deeply affected."[23] In BJ Changhyun's mukbang broadcasts, the viewer messages appear in the upper right corner of his videos. One particular

Korean mukbang wave 87

show posted on YouTube on June 3rd, 2015, which I will examine in depth, has 2,240 accumulated views (as of October 3rd, 2019). The show is titled "Roulette Mission Mukbang."[24] Just as in a game of roulette, BJ Changhyun spins a wheel placed behind his mukbang table and carries out a range of missions while also eating a big portion of extremely spicy *dukboggi*, a popular Korean dish of rice cakes in red pepper paste sauce.

As BJ Changhyun starts and continues his show, viewers simultaneously post their comments addressed either to him or to fellow viewers. BJ Changhyun constantly looks at the screen to read and respond to these comments. He also uses the "finder" function of the broadcasting software and types in keywords when he needs to locate a specific viewer and his/her comment. During the show, a viewer named "Soo" asks BJ Changhyun to dance to a song, "Careless Whisper." He turns on the music and asks, "Is this the song you are talking about?" Another viewer says, "You are eating so much spicy dukboggi in the middle of the night! Your stomach must really hurt. Please take some medicine to sooth your stomach." BJ Changhyun immediately responds: "That is so considerate of you to worry about me!" The music in the background continues, and viewers start making more requests as they wait for BJ Changhyun to start dancing to the song in a comical manner. As he dances, viewers start giving him "star balloons," a type of proprietary virtual currency that can be converted into regular cash. More viewers donate balloons to BJ Changhyun, and he calls out the name of each donor to thank them. In the meantime more chat messages are posted: "Today's show is really fun"; "Your dukboggi looks so delicious and makes me hungry!" "You look so cute with your hair pulled up like that"; and so forth. BJ Changhyun, who is wearing a sleeveless shirt, asks his viewers, "Can I go and change my shirt?" After this question, he leaves his mukbang table (in the meantime, viewers talk to one another) and then comes back shortly with a new shirt. He then says, "That is it for today. I made you laugh enough tonight. You know, I am doing all this with a sole purpose of making you laugh." BJ Changhyun's mukbang show ends there.

Understanding digital media's new dynamics between author/producer/entertainer and reader/consumer/fan

Literary scholars (especially of narrative theory) theorize and define what narrative is in many different ways and with different emphases. Rhetorical theorists, for instance, conceptualize narrative as "somebody telling somebody else that something happened" and focus on "the multilayered communications that authors of narrative offer their audiences, communications that invite or even require their audiences to engage with them cognitively, psychically, emotionally, and ethically."[25] Cognitive theorists, on the other hand, offer yet another approach to narrative with a process of the audience's mental simulations in mind. For them, narratives represent "worlds that are populated with characters and situated in space and time."[26] These scholars are particularly concerned with the "worlds" evoked by narratives and call them "storyworlds," which can be understood as "mental models of who did what to and with whom, when, where, why, and in what fashion in the world to which recipients relocate."[27] While the conceptualization of narrative differs from theorist to theorist, what is common among these diverging views is that the author (narrative producer) and the audience (narrative recipient) are almost always distinctively positioned in two opposing poles of the spectrum: the author on one end as someone who creates, orchestrates, and influences, and the audience on the opposite end as someone who perceives, engages, processes, and relocates. The author is often endowed with god-like characteristics and controls the meaning and interpretation of narrative, whereas his/her audience is expected to "entertain an image of the author as an intentional creator when processing a narrative"[28] and, cognitively speaking, decipher the narrative based on the author's "frames and scripts."[29]

This hierarchical and restrictive binary positioning between media/narrative producer and consumer is, however, "too small, too tight, too circumscribed,"[30] as the interactivity between BJ Changhyun and his viewers clearly evinces. After all, the most defining characteristics of popular culture are "the interactive relationships between consumer and producer, rejecting the mass culture approach that accepted the audience as passive receptors."[31] The changing dynamics in the role of the audience is even more evident in popular culture using a digital platform. Marie-Laure Ryan, for instance, considers this profoundly and introduces a typology of audience position in digital media. According to Ryan, the audience of digital media can take either an internal position or an external position and be involved at the level that is exploratory or ontological. In the internal position, users of media consider themselves as members of the world being projected and simulated and take the first-person perspective. In the external mode, by contrast, media users are anchored outside the projected world and "either play the role of a god who controls the fictional world from above, or they conceptualize their activity as a navigating database."[32] When users take on the exploratory mode, on the other hand, their role and influence are quite limited, while in the ontological status, users' decisions can determine "which possible world, and consequently which story, will develop from the situation in which the choice presents itself."[33] Importantly, users of digital media can take multiple positions simultaneously and can also change their roles in the run of the program that they are involved in and in the process of their viewing/playing.

Ryan's theorization of viewer positions in digital media sheds useful light on the interesting complexity and dynamics of the host–viewer interactivity in BJ Changhyun's show, while the specific working of the show (narratological, technical, and cultural) in turn adds more layers to Ryan's model. At the first glance, viewers of the "Roulette Mission Mukbang" episode seem to take on an external ontological position. This positioning is in part due to the widely adopted convention of mukbang broadcasting that aims to present excessive and dramatized eating. As mentioned earlier, the typical mukbang episode involves either large quantities of a single item or five or six (or even more) double-portion dishes that are usually considered to be unhealthy. This excessive dramatization of eating seems inevitable given the increasing number of mukbang shows in Korea and the severe competition among them.[34] In order to stand out and draw attention from more viewers, each mukbang host chooses to become more "provocative, sensational, and self-abusive."[35] Hyejin Kim, for instance, notices that many popular mukbang hosts select food that is extremely spicy or hot. They also openly express pains and agonies by consuming large quantities of food within a very short time frame. In other words, what happens in mukbang shows can be utterly unappealing, unpleasant, and aversive to watch. Similarly, BJ Changhyun's choice of food for the episode includes a huge portion of a particular type of dukboggi that is specifically known to be extremely spicy. During the show, he often talks about how spicy the dukboggi is, and his discomfort is clear as he frequently speaks about it and as his sweaty face turns red. It is a view that is in fact quite uncomfortable to watch. The best way to derive pleasure from viewing something so aversive as this may be by watching it from a position that is, borrowing Ryan's typology, external rather than internal.

The self-abusive, excessive, and disturbing behaviors of mukbang hosts, in other words, can entertain viewers because viewers' external positioning offers them a safe vantage point from where they can experience the very same actions and behaviors vicariously without having to exercise them from a view point of an intimate insider. That is exactly how literature works, too. Ryan elaborates that our participation in the plot as readers is "a compromise between the first-person and the third-person perspective." We as readers imagine and even transport ourselves into the minds of fictional characters and the fictional world, "but we remain at the same time conscious of being external observers." This ability to take the outside observer position is how readers can separate "pleasure from pain."[36] Viewer commentaries in BJ Changhyun's show capture how viewers maintain the boundary that separates them externally from the world that his show simulates. For instance, one viewer says, "Your stomach must really hurt. You should go and take some *galpos* (popular medicine in Korea to sooth an upset stomach)." The viewer is clearly aware of the host's pain but continues to witness that pain by adopting the third-person perspective and setting up a clear distinction between himself and the host, the second person "you." Simultaneously, the viewer assumes the role of the all-knowing god who, "from above," is able to make a diagnostic, didactic suggestion to the host about what he should do as someone who is internally positioned inside the show.

Other comments, however, reveal that these viewers concurrently maintain a strong desire to occupy the internal first-person position even as they situate themselves outside the show. Viewers say, for instance, "Looking at your show makes me hungry"; "I wish I could also eat dukboggi right now"; and "It must be really spicy, but tasty, too!" Of course, this internal first-person perspective is inseparable from the external third-person perspective—after all, the viewers' move toward the external position originates from their need to experience in first-person what they view without having to actually confront negative consequences of it (that is, the weight gain and stomach pain caused by excessive eating in the middle of the late night). The compromise that viewers make in their third-person position, however, is compensated by the ontological status that the affordances of the digital medium offer to viewers. In a more conventional narrative environment (print media, for instance), where the author produces narrative and the reader consumes it, authorial authority lies in his/her ability to structure and manage a plot (thereby dictating readers' experience of reading), as plot is traditionally considered to be either "as the fixed pattern that will have emerged at the end of the narrative, or as a dynamic development in the progress of the narrative."[37] Although the "dynamic development" implicitly hints at the possibility of readers contributing to the shaping of the plot, readers' involvement in this "dynamic development" is ultimately the result of the author's multilayered communications to readers and is orchestrated specifically by the author himself/herself with an intention to advance the narrative in particular ways. By contrast, in interactive digital media, the plot (media content) is never fixed and instead changes constantly, since digital media see the public "not as simply consumers of pre-constructed messages but as people who are shaping, sharing, reframing and remixing media content in ways which might not have been previously imagined."[38] Plot in digital media is unpredictable, freely disseminated and transformed, and places greater emphasis on the participation of media recipients, that is, the interactivity between media producer and consumer.

Interactivity can be defined as "the repeated interaction of mutually modifying elements that produces non-linear complexity out of simple rules."[39] BJ Changhyun and his viewers operate as these very "mutually modifying elements" and co-produce non-linear narratives (verbal and written) and behaviors that are neither fixed nor pre-structured, but improvise constantly. Viewers of the show make specific requests to BJ Changhyun ("Please bring the food closer to the camera," and "Please dance to the song," for instance), and these requests are reflected in the host's emerging behaviors (the host dancing) and the narratives of both parties (BJ Changhyun saying, "I feel so awkward to dance in front of a camera"; viewers responding, "You are not only a good eater, but also a good dancer!"). Meanwhile, he is not completely dependent on his viewers and, instead, maintains a degree of autonomy and authority. BJ Changhyun is the one who initiates and models viewers' participation and requests—he asks his viewers to suggest a song, to which he will eventually dance, and among the many suggestions he receives, he picks one specific song proposed by one specific viewer. In other words, "[i]n choosing one suggestion from a pool of many, [the host] exerts his own agency."[40] The interactive, spontaneous, and fluid construction of narratives and behaviors in the show signals that neither BJ Changhyun's authorial agency nor viewers' ontological status is absolute and definitive. This duet-dance, oscillating between the host and viewers, is further reinforced by the commercial structure within which mukbang broadcasts operate. Many popular mukbang hosts on Afreeca TV make money through the "star balloons." No viewer is required to pay star balloons to the host, but many voluntarily do so to encourage the host to choose their requests among many others in the pool. Likewise, the host does not have to shape his behavior and narrative according to viewer suggestions, but he/she is more likely to do so with an expectation that a response to viewers will be rewarded by the star balloons that are likely to be offered in return. Indeed, some of the top-ranked mukbang hosts in Korea make as much as $10,000 a month through these viewer donations alone.[41]

The interactivity emerges not only between the host and viewers, but also among viewers themselves. For instance, as a viewer named "dudrnxoddl" rewards BJ Changhyun with 40 star balloons, he acknowledges his/her active participation and donation by calling out the viewer's name and also thanking him/her openly. What is particularly interesting to note, however, is that this viewer's act of donation triggers responses from fellow viewers as well: they, too, acknowledge this particular viewer's engagement with the show and BJ Changhyun by typing in the chat box positive discourse markers such as "oh," "wow," "very generous," and so forth. It is also evident that viewers imitate and motivate each other's behaviors and narratives. Right after "dudrnxoddl" gives his/her balloons, more viewers follow the same step and donate balloons to BJ Changhyun. The host calls out each one of these viewers and emphasizes that he is doing all the "silly things" in order to make them "happy."

Viewer comments and behaviors as well as the ways in which they respond to one another within the chat box echo how fandom/fan community functions. One of the promises of the Internet is "that it can bring together isolated, but like-minded people," regardless of time and space, in order for them to support each other and generate meaning and values among themselves.[42] Whereas the earlier stage of digital media studies focused primarily on the interactivity between media producer and consumer, more recent attention has been paid to the dynamics within fan communities in an attempt to better understand the fandom phenomenon and its impact on media production and consumption more generally. Fandom can be understood as "a vibrant, socially rewarding space where groups of people come together to share interests, ideas, and occasionally work to change the world."[43] What stands out in this definition is the conceptualization of fandom as a "social" space. The identity of the individuals (fans and viewers) belonging to this space, then, can be constructed and reinforced by the shared interests, customs, and values of the community. This further implies that members of fan communities develop certain expectations for each other about how one should behave and act within the given social space and its rules and standards and, consequently, "fans [in fandom] are judged on their ability to engage with the source of their shared passion."[44] These expectations and judgments help maintain the shared identity of the fandom and further strengthen their sense of community and unity.

In the case of BJ Changhyun's mukbang show, the viewer–viewer interaction within the chat box, the fandom-like communal space for the viewers, reflects this shared sociality. Viewers participate and make requests in accordance with the expectations that they communally share as fans of BJ Changhyun's show. Members of the chat box judge individual viewers' actions and narratives, and their ability to engage with BJ Changhyun is publicly evaluated and encouraged (as reflected by such discourse markers as "wow" and "generous of you!"). One member's behavior and narrative impact those of others (once one viewer donates star balloons, more viewers imitate this action and start donating star balloons), and these mutual interactions and feedback loop lead to the strengthening of their network and, ultimately, fandom as participatory culture. The overall consequences are many: new narratives and behaviors emerge not only between the host and viewers but also among viewers, thereby expanding the overall corpus of narrative and narrative universe to investigate; a strong sense of community is established between the host and viewers and among viewers, and mukbang ultimately offers an interesting context for virtual sociality and fandom study. As Dorothy Wai Sim Lau, in "Star Construction in the Era of Media Convergence: Pro-Am Online Videos, Co-creative Culture, and Transnational Chinese Icons on YouTube" posits, the "[p]roliferating, synergistic Web 2.0 platforms like YouTube and Facebook have made possible the 'ever expanding terrain of the amateur.'"[45] Korean mukbang shows participate in this "ever expanding terrain" of amateur visual production and challenge the hegemony of traditional mechanisms of media/narrative production and consumption conceptualized within the strict, hierarchical binary structure of who produces and disseminates versus who consumes and perceives.

My analysis in this chapter has shown how the interactivity between host and viewers and among viewers impacts formation and emergence of narratives and behaviors in mukbang broadcasting. Additionally, it is clear that the interaction among viewers in the chat box is the result of the virtual sociality that mukbang's fandom-like community establishes for its viewers. Indeed, this viewer–viewer interaction adds an extra layer to the narrative production and consumption of the show. Mukbang shows also present a case where amateur digital media production constructs a relatively profitable commercial cultural space. It should be noted that both the mukbang host and viewers use this commercial structure of the show to advance their own respective interests. The mukbang host willingly grants more authority to his/her viewers by closely reading viewers' suggestions and requests and acting accordingly, with the expectation that viewers will reward his response through their economic means, the star balloons. Viewers actively exercise the authority given to them and make requests with an understanding that the more generous they are, the more responsive the host will be to them. Undoubtedly, this commercial structure of mukbang shows is a sad reflection of the capitalism and the ways in which it dictates how we as human beings think, feel, act, and interact within society at large (virtual and actual). It still feels uncommon that people live-stream themselves overeating in front of a camera. It is absurd and even disturbing that viewers spend their time watching such live-stream videos and even pay money to see the host eat, dance, or bring food closer to the camera for a better view. Nevertheless, the cultural, narratological, and technical considerations given to mukbang in this chapter help make sense of the why and how of such a strange modern phenomenon. The popularity and global spread of mukbang, then, contribute to the understanding of multiple facets of who and what we are, how and why we produce and consume media and narrative, and how they inform us and others across boundaries.

Notes

1 Hyesu Park, "Media, Narrative, and Culture: Narrativizing and Contextualizing Korean Mukbang Shows," in *Media Culture in Transnational Asia: Convergences and Divergences*, ed. Hyesu Park (New Brunswick: Rutgers University Press, 2020), 129–147.
2 My use of text in this chapter (and in any other chapter) is not exclusively linguistically defined, but refers to "any expression that can be read or otherwise experienced as meaningful." See Liv Hausken, "Textual Theory and Blind Spots in Media Studies," in *Narrative across Media: The Languages of Storytelling*, ed. Marie-Laure Ryan (Lincoln: University of Nebraska, 2004), 392.
3 Ibid., 397.
4 Marie-Laure Ryan, "Will New Media Produce New Narratives?" in *Narrative Across Media: The Languages of Storytelling*, ed. Marie-Laure Ryan (Lincoln: University of Nebraska, 2004), 337.
5 Ibid.
6 See Ryan, "Will New Media," 338 for more detailed discussion on the fundamental properties of digital media.
7 Amy McCarthy, "This Korean Food Phenomenon Is Changing the Internet," *Eater.com*, last modified April 19, 2017, www.eater.com/2017/4/19/15349568/mukbang-videos-korean-youtube.
8 Pauline Adema, "Vicarious Consumption: Food, Television and the Ambiguity of Modernity," *Journal of American Culture* 23, no. 3 (2000): 113–123.
9 Ibid., 120.
10 Ibid., 113.
11 *KOSIS*, Korean Statistical Information Service, accessed January 11, 2019, http://kosis.kr/eng/index/index.do.
12 Youna Kim, "Media Globalization in Asia," in *Media Consumption and Everyday Life in Asia*, ed. Youna Kim (New York: Routledge, 2008), 12.
13 How mukbang viewers communicate with the host and fellow viewers will be further discussed in the later section of the chapter where I analyze the case study.

14 Hanwool Choe, "Eating Together Multimodally: Collaborative Eating in Mukbang, a Korean Livestream of Eating," *Language in Society* 48 (2019): 174.
15 The term "lookism," referring to a discriminatory treatment toward people considered physically unattractive, was first coined in the 1970s and used in *The Washington Post* magazine in 1978. The word now appears in several major English-language dictionaries.
16 "South Korea Has the Lowest Overweight among all the OECD nations, but!" (my trans.), *Joongang Ilbo* online, last modified January 23, 2015, https://news.joins.com/article/17010069.
17 Kim, "Media," 3.
18 For example, if one types "Indian mukbang" on YouTube, numerous video clips uploaded by Indians show up, wherein they eat either Korean food or Indian food and talking to their viewers.
19 There are, however, some distinct cultural differences between Korean and American mukbang shows. In Korean mukbang broadcasts, hosts are usually silent or talk about the food that they consume, whereas American hosts in American mukbang broadcasts share personal thoughts and feelings (the stream-of-consciousness commentary), which are often irrelevant to the food that they eat. See www.eater.com/2017/4/19/15349568/mukbang-videos-korean-youtube.
20 Kagan Kircaburun, Andrew Harris, Filipa Calado, and Mark Griffiths. "The Psychology of Mukbang Watching: A Scoping Review of the Academic and Non-academic Literature," *International Journal of Mental Health and Addiction*, January 6, 2020, http://doi.org/10.1007/s11469-019-00211-0.
21 Ibid.
22 ASMR University, "The Arts & Science of Autonomous Sensory Meridian Response," accessed June 2, 2020, https://asmruniversity.com.
23 Ryan, "Will New Media," 339.
24 BJ Changhyun, "Roulette Mission Mukbang," *YouTube*, June 3, 2015, www.youtube.com/watch?v=XZ5CPynvWdw&t=465s.
25 James Phelan, *Living to Tell About It* (Ithaca: Cornell University Press, 2005), 5.
26 David Herman, *Story Logic* (Lincoln: University of Nebraska Press, 2002), 9.
27 Ibid.
28 Luc Herman, "The Implied Author: A Secular Excommunication," *Style* 45, no. 1 (2011): 14.
29 Ibid.
30 Susan Lanser, "(Im)plying the Author," *Narrative* 9, no. 2 (2001): 158. [153–160].
31 Adema, "Vicarious," 114. Consumption: Food.
32 Ryan, "Will new media," 339.
33 Ibid.
34 In 2015, there were 3,000 active mukbang hosts in Korea with one or more shows regularly updated. The number has most likely increased

since then. See Elise Hu, "Koreans Have an Insatiable Appetite for watching Strangers Binge Eat," *NPR*, March 24, 2015 (3:36 a.m. ET), www.npr.org/sections/thesalt/2015/03/24/392430233/koreans-have-an-insatiable-appetite-for-watching-strangers-binge-eat.
35 Hyejin Kim, "Investigation of *Mukbang* as a Lowbrow Cultural Phenomenon as Well as Food Pornography" (my trans.), *Journal of Humanities Studies* 50 (2015): 441.
36 Ryan, "Will New Media," 347.
37 Hanna-Riikka Roine, "Computational Media and the Core Concepts of Narrative Theory," *Narrative* 27, no. 3 (2019): 321.
38 Henry Jenkins, Sam Ford, and Joshua Green, *Spreadable Media: Creating Value and Meaning in a Networked Culture* (New York: New York University Press, 2013), 2.
39 Richard Walsh, "Emergent Narrative in Interactive Media," *Narrative* 19, no. 1 (2011): 76.
40 Choe, "Eating," 183.
41 According to an *NPR* article, some top-ranked Mukbang hosts earn up to $10,000 a month. See Elise Hu, "Koreans Have an Insatiable Appetite for watching Strangers Binge Eat," *NPR*, March 24, 2015 (3:36 a.m. ET), www.npr.org/sections/thesalt/2015/03/24/392430233/koreans-have-an-insatiable-appetite-for-watching-strangers-binge-eat.
42 Matthew Guschwan, "New Media: Online Fandom," *Soccer & Society* 17, no. 3 (2016): 352
43 Jessica Seymour, Alice Chauvel, and Nicolle Lamerichs, "Introduction," in *Fan Studies: Researching Popular Audiences*, ed. Jessica Seymour, Alice Chauvel, and Nicolle Lamerichs (Manchester: Inter-Disciplinary Press, 2014), i.
44 Ibid.
45 Dorothy Wai Sim Lau, "Star Construction in the Era of Media Convergence: Pro-Am Online Videos, Co-creative Culture, and Transnational Chinese Icons on YouTube," in *Media Culture in Transnational Asia: Convergences and Divergences*, ed. Hyesu Park (New Brunswick: Rutgers University Press, 2020), 63.

Bibliography

ASMR University. "The Arts & Science of Autonomous Sensory Meridian Response." Accessed June 2, 2020. https://asmruniversity.com.
Changhyun, BJ. "Roulette Mission Mukbang." *YouTube*. June 3, 2015. www.youtube.com/watch?v=XZ5CPynvWdw&t=465s.
Choe, Hanwool. "Eating Together Multimodally: Collaborative Eating in Mukbang, a Korean Livestream of Eating." *Language in Society* 48 (2019): 171–208.
Guschwan, Matthew. "New Media: Online Fandom." *Soccer & Society* 17, no. 3 (2016): 351–371.

Hausken, Liv. "Textual Theory and Blind Spots in Media Studies." In *Narrative Across Media: The Languages of Storytelling*, edited by Marie-Laure Ryan, 391–403. Lincoln: University of Nebraska, 2004.
Herman, David. *Story Logic*. Lincoln: University of Nebraska Press, 2002.
Herman, Luc. "The Implied Author: A Secular Excommunication." *Style* 45, no. 1 (2011): 11–28.
Hu, Elise. "Koreans Have an Insatiable Appetite for watching Strangers Binge Eat." *NPR*. March 24, 2015 (3:36 a.m. ET). www.npr.org/sections/thesalt/2015/03/24/392430233/koreans-have-an-insatiable-appetite-for-watching-strangers-binge-eat.
Jenkins, Henry, Sam Ford, and Joshua Green. *Spreadable Media: Creating Value and Meaning in a Networked Culture*. New York: New York University Press, 2013.
Kim, Hyejin. "Investigation of *Mukbang* as a Lowbrow Cultural Phenomenon as Well as Food Pornography." [my trans.] *Journal of Humanities Studies* 50 (2015): 433–455.
Kim, Youna. "Media Globalization in Asia." In *Media Consumption and Everyday Life in Asia*, edited by Youna Kim, 1–24. New York: Routledge, 2008.
Kircaburun, Kagan, Andrew Harris, Filipa Calado, and Mark Griffiths. "The Psychology of Mukbang Watching: A Scoping Review of the Academic and Non-academic Literature." *International Journal of Mental Health and Addiction*. January 6, 2020. http://doi.org/10.1007/s11469-019-00211-0.
KOSIS. Korean Statistical Information Service. Accessed January 11, 2019. http://kosis.kr/eng/index/index.do.
Lanser, Susan. "(Im)plying the Author." *Narrative* 9, no. 2 (2001): 153–160.
Lau, Dorothy Wai Sim. "Star Construction in the Era of Media Convergence: Pro-Am Online Videos, Co-creative Culture, and Transnational Chinese Icons on YouTube." In *Media Culture in Transnational Asia: Convergences and Divergences*, edited by Hyesu Park, 54–71. New Brunswick: Rutgers University Press, 2020.
McCarthy, Amy. "This Korean Food Phenomenon Is Changing the Internet." *Eater.com*. Last modified April 19, 2017. www.eater.com/2017/4/19/15349568/mukbang-videos-korean-youtube.
Park, Hyesu. "Media, Narrative, and Culture: Narrativizing and Contextualizing Korean Mukbang Shows." In *Media Culture in Transnational Asia: Convergences and Divergences*, edited by Hyesu Park, 129–147. New Brunswick: Rutgers University Press, 2020.
Pauline Adema, Pauline. "Vicarious Consumption: Food, Television and the Ambiguity of Modernity." *Journal of American Culture* 23, no.3 (2000): 113–123.
Phelan, James Phelan. *Living to Tell About It*. Ithaca: Cornell University Press, 2005.
Roine, Hanna-Riikka. "Computational Media and the Core Concepts of Narrative Theory." *Narrative* 27, no. 3 (2019): 331–331.

Ryan, Marie-Laure. "Will New Media Produce New Narratives?" In *Narrative Across Media: The Languages of Storytelling*, edited by Marie-Laure Ryan, 337–359. Lincoln: University of Nebraska, 2004.

Seymour, Jessica, Alice Chauvel, and Nicolle Lamerichs. "Introduction." In *Fan Studies: Researching Popular Audiences*, edited by Jessica Seymour, Alice Chauvel, and Nicolle Lamerichs, i-vii. Manchester: Inter-Disciplinary Press, 2014.

"South Korea Has the Lowest Overweight among All OECD Nations, but!" [my trans.] *Joongang Ilbo* online. Last modified January 23, 2015. https://news.joins.com/article/17010069.

Walsh, Richard. "Emergent Narrative in Interactive Media." *Narrative* 19, no. 1 (2011): 72–85.

Index

Abbott, Porter 29, 64–5
adaptation 7, 55, 75
Adema, Pauline 83
Afreeca TV 16, 81–6
Amygdala 63
Ancco: Bad Friend 36–9, 40–3
Angoulême International Comics Festival 36
Asia: as method 4
augmented reality 16, 54, 72
audience: authorial 13–14
autobiographical: ofnarration 26; of narrator 43
autographics 37
Autonomous Sensory Motor Response (ASMR) 86

bad taste webtoon 61–2
Beard, James 83
BJ Changhyun 82, 86–9
Bolter, Jay Bolter 55; *see also* remediation
BTS 4–5
Butler, Judith 37
Butte, George 59

Caracciolo, Marco 69, 71
Cartoon 39, 41
Castells, Manuel 7; *see also* networked society
Chen, KuanHsing 4
Chute, Hillary 37
closure: of comics 37
co-create culture 9
cognitive: of theory 14

coming-of-age story 36
communalism 32
compressed modernity 3
Confucian virtue 32
cross-cultural: acceptance 11; exchanges 11; studies 12

defamiliarization: of literary 65
deictic features 69
digital: digital comics 1, 66; digital media 12, 14, 16; digital revolution model 55
digitalization: of Korea 1
Dittmar, Jakob 66
Dr. P Series 59–60

ecofeminism 15
embedded narrative 34, 36; *see also* private text
embodied reading 54, 68–9; *see also* experiential reading
empathy 37, 60–1
experiential reading 68
experientiality 72–3
exploratory: of audience position 88
external position: of audience 88

facial recognition technology 68, 71–2
fan: behaviors 13; networks 10
fandom 12–13
feminist: of narratology 26; of perspective 28; reading 32–3
focalization: external focalization 30, 38; internal focalization 30, 35
food anxiety 84–5

Gangnam style 4
Genette, Gerald: Narrative Discourse 38
globalization 1, 4, 13, 20
graphic: of memoir 25–6, 36–9; of narrative 15, 26
Gross Domestic Product (GDP) 3
group identity 6
Grusin, Richard 55
guilty pleasure 62
gutter: of comics 31, 41, 44–5, 66

Hemenover, Scott 63
Herman, David 14, 69
Hirsch, Marianne 37
Hogan, Patrick 6

identity: categories of 7; cultural 7; of group 6
implied reader 32–3
individualism 83
infinite canvas 66, 74
inscrutability 29–30, 64–5
interactivity: of media 55
interior monologue 30–1
internal position: of audience position 88–9, 90
intradiegetic 14
Iser, Wolfgang 32
Iversen, Stefan 65

Jenkins, Henry 9, 57, 75–6
Jin, Dal Yong 8

K drama 25
K-pop 4, 6
Kang Full: *Apartment* 56
Kang, Han: *The Vegetarian* 25, 27–9
Kwon, Ha-Il: *Encountered* 68
Keen, Suzanne 37, 60
Kim, Youna 4–5
Korea Information Infrastructure 8
Korean Wave 1–2, 4–5
Kraidy, Marwan 14
Kyung-sook, Shin: *Please Look After Mom* 25

Line Webtoon 53
Lookism 5, 84–5
lyric quality 15, 26

mak-jang 61
manga 53
manhwa 53
Martinez, M. Angeles 70
McCloud, Scott 41, 66, 74
McHale, Brian 30
McLuhan, Marshall 10, 55
media convergence 1, 55, 74
mediality 14, 16
medium 10, 14–15
Melville, Herman: "Bartleby the Scrivener" 64
Metamorphosis 35
Miller, Toby 14
Modernization 3, 42, 85
motion webtoon 66
mukbang 81–9
multiple implied readers 32–3

narratee 30–2, 34
narratology 11–12
Naver 53, 56–8
neo-Confucianism 83; *see also* Confucian virtue
netizen 61
network society 7

online live-streaming platform 16, 81
ontological: of audience position 88–90
Organization for Economic Cooperation and Development (OECD) 3, 5

page layout 43, 67
Palmer, Alan 59
pan-Asian 4
panel: of comics 38–9, 40–1
participatory: activities 58; culture 93
patriarchy 28, 32
perspectival immersion 68
Phelan, James 13, 44, 48
Plot 55, 59, 61
Polyphonic 45
pop Asianism 4
portal platform 58
postmemory 37
postmodern poetics 28
primary narrative 34, 36
private text 31, 34, 36

prosumers 8
Psy 4

Rabinowitz, Peter 42
Remediation 1, 55, 74
Richardson, Brian 32–3
Ryan, Marie-Laure 10, 58

sensorimotorcontingencies 72
Shklovsky, Viktor 65
Siapera, Eugenia 7
SM Entertainment 9
smartphone ownership rates: of Korea 3
Sok-young, Hwang 25
Sontag, Susan 37
Soompi 9
spatial: boundaries 44; immersion 68; make-up 73
Spiegleman, Art: *Maus* 37
star balloons: virtual currency 87, 91–2
storyworlds 14, 30
Sun-mi, Hwang: *The Hen Who Dreamed She Could Fly* 25

techno-mediated: of narrative environment 16, 54

tellability 37
Theory of Mind (ToM) 59–60
thought balloons 38; *see also* word balloons
transcultural fandom 12
transmedia storytelling 54–5

universality 6, 33, 41
unnatural narrative 26–7
User Create Contents (UCC) 61

vantage point 36, 39, 89
vicarious consumption: of food 83–5
visual narrative 37–8

Walton, Kendall 69
Web 2.0 platforms 93
Webtoon 53–9
Whitlock, Gillian 37
word balloons 38

YG Entertainment 9
YouTube 4, 8–10

Zunshine, Lisa: *Why We Read Fiction* 59–60

For Product Safety Concerns and Information please contact our EU representative GPSR@taylorandfrancis.com
Taylor & Francis Verlag GmbH, Kaufingerstraße 24, 80331 München, Germany

www.ingramcontent.com/pod-product-compliance
Lightning Source LLC
Chambersburg PA
CBHW051757230426
43670CB00012B/2333